河南省南水北调工程

考古发掘出土文物集萃（一）

河南省文物局

文物出版社

责任印制：张道奇

责任编辑：王　伟

图书在版编目（CIP）数据

　　河南省南水北调工程考古发掘出土文物集萃．1/河南
省文物局编．－北京：文物出版社，2009.2
　　ISBN 978-7-5010-2482-7

　　Ⅰ．河…　Ⅱ．河…　Ⅲ．南水北调－水利工程－出土文物－
河南省－图集　Ⅳ．K873.61

　　中国版本图书馆CIP数据核字（2008）第067904号

河南省南水北调工程考古发掘出土文物集萃（一）

编　　者　河南省文物局
出版发行　文物出版社
地　　址　北京市东直门内北小街2号楼
　　　　　100007
　　　　　http://www.wenwu.com
　　　　　web@wenwu.com

制版印刷　北京燕泰美术制版印刷有限责任公司
经　　销　新华书店
版　　次　2009年2月第1版第1次印刷
开　　本　889×1194　　1/16
印　　张　15
书　　号　ISBN 978-7-5010-2482-7
定　　价　298.00元

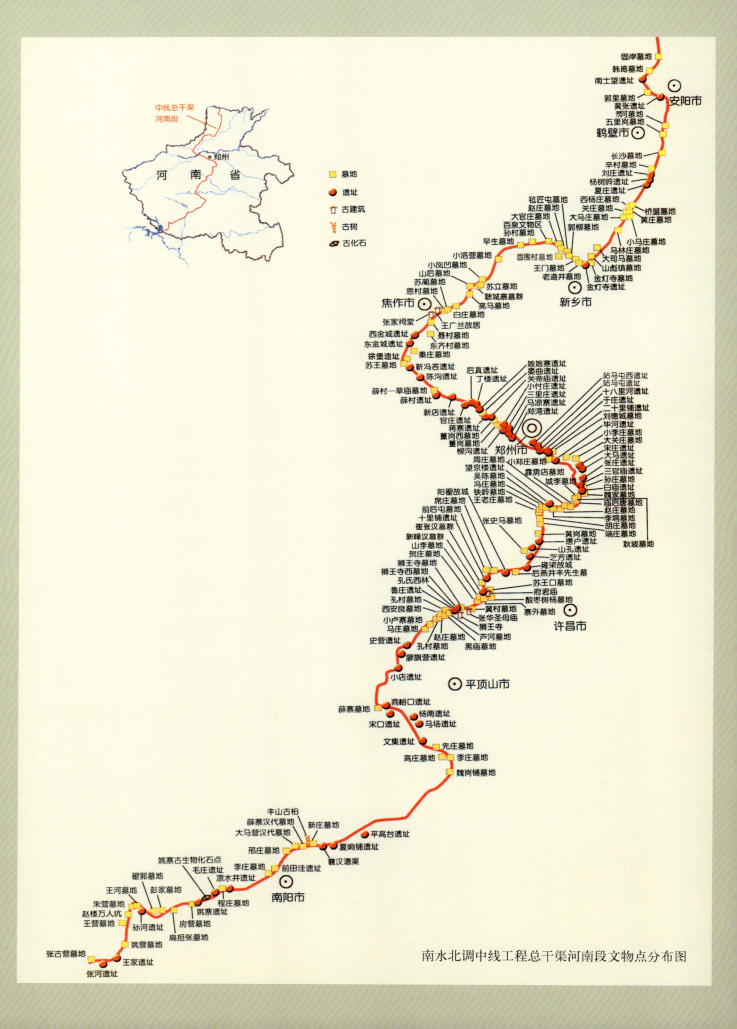

中线总干渠
河南段

河南省

郑州

墓地
遗址
古建筑
古树
古化石

固岸墓地
韩崎墓地
南士望遗址
安阳市
郭里墓地
黄张遗址
郗墓地
五里岗墓地
鹤壁市

长沙墓地
辛村墓地
刘庄遗址
杨树岭遗址
夏庄遗址
毡匠屯墓地   西杨庄墓地
赵庄墓地   关庄墓地   桥盟墓地
大官庄墓地   大马庄墓地   黄墓墓地
百泉文物区   郭柳墓地
孙村墓地   小马庄墓地
早生墓地   马林庄墓地
小洛营墓地   固围村墓地   大司马墓地
小凤凹墓地   王门墓地   山彪镇墓地
山后墓地   老道井墓地   金灯寺墓地
苏蘭墓地   苏立墓地   金灯寺遗址
恩村墓地   聊城寨墓群
焦作市   亮马寨墓地
                  白庄墓地
张家祠堂   王广兰故居
西金城遗址   聂村墓地
东金城遗址   东齐村墓地
徐堡遗址   秦庄墓地   后真遗址   娘娘寨遗址
苏王墓地   新冯昝遗址   丁楼遗址   荥曲遗址   站马屯西遗址
                  陈沟遗址   关帝庙遗址   站马屯遗址
薛村一草庙墓地   小忖庄遗址   十八里河遗址
薛村遗址   三里庄遗址   于庄遗址
                  新店遗址   马凉寨遗址   二十里铺遗址
                  官庄遗址   郑湾遗址   刘德庄墓地
                  蒋寨遗址   毕河遗址
                  董岗西墓地   小李庄墓地
                  董岗墓地   郑州市   大关庄墓地
                  柳沟遗址   宋庄遗址
                  周口楼遗址   小郑庄遗址   大马遗址
                  望京楼遗址   张庄遗址
                  吴陈墓地   轟雾店墓地   三官庙遗址
                  冯庄墓地   城李墓地   孙庄墓地
阳翟故城   铁岭墓地   白庙遗址
席庄墓地   王老庄墓地   魏家墓地
前后屯墓地   庙后唐墓地
十里铺遗址   张史马墓地   赵庄墓地
崔张汉墓群   李桐遗址
新峰汉墓群   黄岗墓地   胡庄墓地   端庄墓地
山李墓地   唐户遗址   耿坡墓地
贺庄墓地   山孔遗址
狮王寺墓地   芝芳遗址
狮王寺西墓地   雍梁故城
孔氏西林   后燕井丰先生墓
鲁庄遗址   苏王口墓地
孔村墓地   一冀村墓地   府君庙
西安良墓地   张华圣母庙   酸枣树杨墓地
小卢寨墓地   狮王寺   寨外墓地
马庄墓地   赵庄墓地   许昌市
史营遗址   孔村墓地   芦河墓地
廖旗营遗址   黑庙墓地
                小店遗址   平顶山市
薛寨墓地   商峪口遗址
                宋口遗址   杨南遗址
                              马场遗址
                文集遗址   先庄墓地
                高庄墓地   李庄墓地
                              魏岗铺墓地

丰山古柏
薛寨汉代墓地   新庄墓地
大马营汉代墓地   平高台遗址
                邢庄墓地   夏响铺遗址
姚寨古生物化石点 毛庄遗址   襄汉漕渠
翟郭墓地   李庄墓地
彭家墓地   凉水井遗址   前田洼遗址
王河墓地   南阳市
朱营墓地   程庄墓地
赵楼万人坑   孙河遗址
王营墓地   房营墓地
                扁担张墓地
张古营墓地   姚营墓地
        王家遗址
    张河遗址

南水北调中线工程总干渠河南段文物点分布图

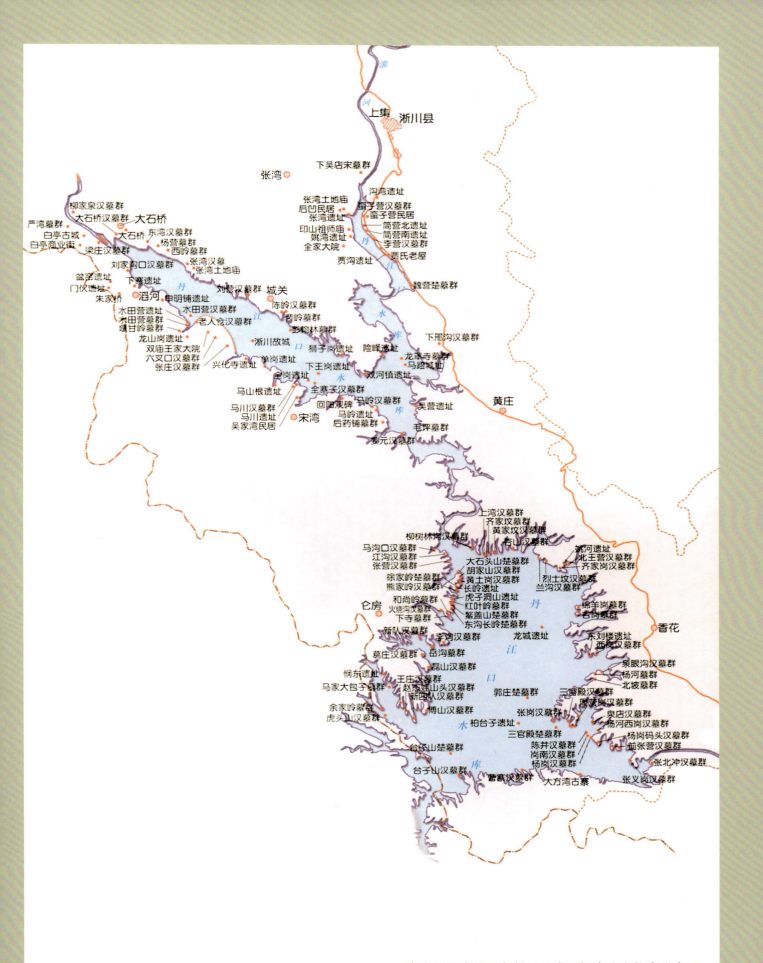

南水北调中线工程丹江口库区河南省文物点分布图

目　录
CONTENTS

序

中共河南省委常委　宣传部长　　
河南省政府副省长　　　　　　　孔玉芳

　　文物是历史与文明传承的重要载体，是不可再生的宝贵文化遗产，文物保护是南水北调工程建设的重要组成部分。做好南水北调工程的文物保护工作，对于传承民族文化、推进社会主义先进文化建设意义重大，是历史赋予我们义不容辞的责任。

　　河南历史悠久、文化灿烂，是中华民族和中华文明的主要发祥地之一。历史上河南曾长期是中国政治、经济、文化中心，中国八大古都，河南有4个：九朝古都洛阳、七朝古都开封、殷商古都安阳和商代都城郑州。河南文化遗产丰富，地下文物居全国第一位，馆藏文物占全国的八分之一。在南水北调中线工程涉及的5个省市中，地下文物埋藏最为丰富，文物保护工作量也最大。南水北调中线工程总干渠穿过郑州、安阳两大古都，经过卫辉山彪墓地、辉县百泉墓地、新郑唐户遗址、新郑胡庄墓地等四处全国盘点文物保护单位。南水北调中线工程建设中的文物抢救保护工作对河南乃至全国现有的文物保护措施和技术手段都提出了新的更高的要求，也为河南省文物事业发展提供了重要契机。

　　河南省委、省政府高度重视南水北调中线工程文物保护工作，在人力、物力、财力上给予了积极支持，保证了文物抢救保护工作正常开展。河南省文物管理局及参与南水北调工程文物抢救性发掘的专家学者和文物工作者，积极探索新形势下文物保护工作的新思路，高标准、高质量、创造性地开展文物保护抢救工作，有效地保护了文物，有力地推动了工程建设的顺利进行。目前已完成82个文物保护项目的考古发掘工作，出土文物3万余件，其中，鹤壁刘庄遗址、安阳固岸遗址、荥阳关帝庙遗址、新郑唐户遗址等四个项目入选年度"全国十大考古新发现"。

　　南水北调工程文物保护工作已度过了三年光荣而艰辛的历程，取得了非凡的成就。这次，河南率先举办考古成果展并出版图录，为展示南水北调工程文物保护工作成果开辟了新的窗口。希望全省各级文物部门以十七大精神为指导，深入贯彻落实科学发展观，再接再厉，开拓进取，认真做好文物的发掘、保护和利用工作，为建设文化强省、构建和谐中原做出新的更大的贡献。

Preface

Kong Yufang
*Director, Propaganda Department, Member of Standing
Committee of Henan Province, Chinese Communist Party
Vice-governor of Henan Provincial Government*

Cultural relics are a crucial carrier of history, civilization, and precious irreplaceable cultural heritage. The conservation of cultural relics is a main goal in the Project of Water Diversion from South to North. The conservation of cultural relics is of significance to national culture and promotion of the construction of an advanced socialist society. This is the responsibility that history has entrusted to us.

Henan is one of the cradles of the Chinese nation and civilization, with a long history and a brilliant culture. In Chinese history, Henan has long been the political, economic, and cultural center. China has eight ancient capitals, of which four are located in Henan Province: Luoyang, Kaifeng, Anyang, and Zhengzhou. Henan has a rich cultural and archaeological tradition, which has yielded among the largest numbers of cultural relics stored at museums in all of China. Among the five provinces involved in the Middle-line Project of Water Diversion from South to North, Henan has produced the most archaeological relics and requires the most to be done in the area of conservation. The main channel of the Middle-line Project of Water Diversion from South to North passes through the ancient capitals of Zhengzhou and Anyang, as well as four other historical and cultural monuments under national protection. These include the Shanbiao cemetery in Weihui, the Baiquan cemetery in Huixian, the Tanghu site, and the Huzhuang cemetery in Xinzheng. Salvage and protection of cultural relics during the construction of the Middle-line Project of Water Diversion from South to North has enabled both Henan and China to make use of existing protective measures and techniques, as well as develop new ones.

The government of Henan strongly emphasizes the protection of cultural heritage in the Middle-line Project of Water Diversion from South to North. The government supports this work with manpower, material resources, and direct financial aid. This support ensures the protection of cultural relics. Experts and archaeologists at the Henan Provincial Administration of Cultural Heritage have engaged in salvage excavations and have actively explored new ideas for the protection of cultural relics. Administrators have been effective in the protection of cultural relics, while maintaining the progress of the project. So far, eighty-two excavations have been completed and more than thirty thousand objects have been collected. Of these excavations, four have been honored in the "Top Ten New Archaeological Discoveries in China." The sites so honored are the Liuzhuang site in Hebi, the Gu'an site in Anyang, the Guandimiao site in Xingyang, and the Tanghu site in Xinzheng.

The work done in protecting cultural relics over the past three years during the Project of Water Diversion from South to North has been very successful. Henan is the leader in archaeological achievement and in publications. I hope each branch of cultural heritage in Henan, guided by the spirit of the Seventeenth Conference of the Chinese Communist Party, carries out the scientific development concept and gives the best possible effort to do successful excavation, protection and utilization work, as well as contribute to constructing a strong cultural province and harmonious Central Plain.

河南省南水北调工程

考古发掘出土文物集萃（一）

布密集、排列规律的大面积先商文化墓地，填补了先商文化发掘和研究工作的一

在发掘过程中，不仅注重各类文物的抢救保护，而且采用现代科技手段，最大可能

地采集各类标本。特别是对于出土的人骨、兽骨进行了性别、年龄、病理以及DNA等方面的鉴定；按照国家地理信息标准，对每处文物点都测量绘制了要素齐全的总平面图，为今后文物普查和保护奠定了基础。如武汉大学历史系对辉县大官庄墓地的一座九个墓室的大型汉墓，进行了发掘现场三维重建和近景摄影测绘技术的全面测绘，通过数字测绘技术、计算机虚拟现实技术，建立了三维的考古对象模型；山东大学在博爱西金城遗址发掘中，设立了主要涉及古地貌、动物、植物、石器、陶器以及遗址资源域十余个子课题的环境考古课题，是开展多学科综合研究的一次重大尝试。

河南省南水北调工程文物保护工作度过了艰辛而光荣的历程。我们积极探索大型项目建设中文物保护抢救工作的新路子，更新管理理念，创新管理机制，培育专业队伍，提升研究层次，取得了非凡的荣誉。鹤壁刘庄遗址、安阳固岸遗址、荥阳关帝庙遗址、新郑唐户遗址等四个项目先后入选"全国十大考古新发现"；国家文物局授予河南省文物局南水北调文物保护

办公室 "全国文化遗产保护工作先进集体"荣誉称号，授予鹤壁刘庄遗址、荥阳关帝庙遗址、新郑唐户遗址等三个项目"全国田野考古质量奖"。

河南省南水北调工程文物保护工作一直受到各级领导的关心和社会各界的支持。全国政协张思卿副主席曾率团视察河南省南水北调工程文物保护工作。国务院南水北调办公室和国家文物局各位领导多次亲临一线检查指导，帮助排忧解难。河南省委、省政府多次召开会议，研究解决文物抢救保护工程中的重大问题。国家著名文物考古学家黄景略、张忠培、徐光冀、邹衡、李伯谦等先生多次深入到文物保护抢救现场，对重大学术问题和考古发掘质量给予帮助指导。社会各界特别是新闻媒体给予极大关注和广泛宣传。

在第三个全国"文化遗产日"到来之际，河南省举办南水北调文物考古成果展并出版图录，正是为了展示这一值得纪念的业绩和成果，感谢领导和社会各界的关心支持，同时也为世人了解南水北调文物抢救保护工程打开了一扇令人神往的大门。

Introduction

Chen Ailan
Director of Henan Provincial Administration of Cultural Heritage

The well-known grand project of water conservation and the protection work of cultural relics in the Project of Water Diversion from South to North is unprecedented in Henan. The number of ancient sites examined is unparalleled in the history of Henan archaeology. After finishing the conservation work of cultural relics in Xiaolangdi Reservoir of the Yellow River and Sanxia Reservoir of the Yangtze River, people have begun to focus on designing and constructing the Middle -line Project of Water Diversion from South to North in the Central Plain. An important issue in this project is how to efficiently protect the precious cultural heritage in the Central Plain.

The Middle-line Project of Water Diversion from South to North includes two aspects: the water source area and the main channel. The water source area or Danjiangkou Reservoir, spanning from Henan to Hubei, is a total of 370 km^2 of submerged landscape, of which 170 km^2 is located in Henan (accounting for 46% of the total submerged area). The main channel starts in Taocha, Xichuan county, Henan province and flows through Henan, Hebei, Beijing and Tianjin. The total length of the channel is 1276 km, of which 731 km (or 58%) runs through Henan province. The main channel passes through 8 cities and 34 counties within Henan, from the Nanyang Basin northward along the eastern foot of the Taihang Mountains. The cities are: Nanyang, Pingdingshan, Xuchang, Zhengzhou, Jiaozuo, Xinxiang, Hebi, and Anyang. The project traverses the ancient Central Plain. Sites in the submerged area, along the main channel, and in the surrounding region show evidence of Paleolithic fossil beds, including remains of ancient Homo, and Neolithic settlements, as well as historical city sites, cemeteries, ancient buildings, and carved stone art reflecting different cultural styles and evidence of cultural exchange. This forms an ancient cultural pathway combining various cultural periods and cultural factors.

The conservation of cultural relics along the Middle-line Project of Water Diversion from South to North in Henan has several distinct characteristics:

First, archaeological teams from all over the country have actively participated in the work. From 1994 to 2005, Henan organized teams from archaeological and engineering institutions to survey, check, and verify work on cultural heritage in the Danjiangkou submerged area and along the main channel. As confirmed by the national departments, there are 330 archaeological sites in Henan that relate to the Middle-line Project of Water Diversion from South to North. Related conservation work in Henan formally began in April 2005. The State Administration of Cultural Heritage held the "Mobilization Conference of the Whole Country Supporting the Conservation Work for the Water Diversion Project from South to North" in Zhengzhou in November 2005. A total of 38 archaeological institutions, including the Henan Provincial Institute of Cultural Relics and Archaeology, the Institute of Archaeology, Chinese Academy of Social Sciences, the History Department of Wuhan University, the Shaanxi Provincial Institute of Archaeology, and so on, have participated in the conservation of cultural relics in Henan. The Henan Administration of Cultural Heritage has organized experts to super-

河南省南水北调工程

考古发掘出土文物集萃（一）

vise archaeological fieldwork, and has provided good field conditions for the archaeological teams. This has ensured that the construction of the project and the conservation of cultural relics occur smoothly.

Second, a large number of precious cultural relics have been recovered and protected. The conservation of cultural relics in the Water Diversion Project from South to North is a major task, made more difficult by the openness of the main channel opened, which increases the danger to cultural relics. We have organized archaeological teams to join in the excavation work in advance and effectively protect the cultural relics. As of December 2007, eight-two archaeological programs had been finished, and twenty-eight programs are still underway in Henan province. The excavation area is over 32 ha. in total. More than thirty thousand artifacts have been collected, including many precious cultural relics, such as those recovered in the tomb of a noble from the early Warring States period at the Xujialing cemetery, among them a small ding tripod with 49 clear inscriptions. These inscriptions indicate a year, suixing and identity the deceased individual buried in the tomb. This provides the important information for investigating the time of burial and identifying the dead. A number of beautiful pieces of gold headgear were unearthed from the Qing Dynasty shoubei's tomb at Xi'an Mansion at Guanzhuang cemetery in Hebi. In particular, a golden crest with an imprinted pattern of ascending prunus blossoms has high artistic value. Four Tang tricolor bowls recovered from Niecun cemetery in Boai County are rare high-quality artifacts.

Third, archaeological finds have important scientific research value. For instance, the cemetery at Liuzhuang in Hebi is the first Pre-Shang cemetery uncovered in China, filling a gap in Pre-Shang culture. The cemetery at Gu'an in Anyang revealed the first Eastern Wei stone couch, with a surrounding screen bearing twenty-four filials, as well as the first clearly inscribed date for an Eastern Wei tomb. At the same cemetery, a large number of Northern Qi ceramic figurines, and porcelain vessels, as well as an epitaph dating to the Northern Qi and Eastern Wei, were found. These findings are important in investigating burial systems, ceramic statuary art, the origins and manufacturing techniques of white and black porcelain in the North, and writing from the Northern Qi and Eastern Wei periods. The excavation at the Dasima cemetery in Weihui unearthed a joint burial of a Qifuling couple from the Tang Dynasty and provides new evidence for the bureaucratic system, writing arts, and social bloom in the Sui and Tang Dynasties. The discovery of a Longshan site at Xubao in Wenxian county revealed one of the largest and best preserved cities in the Yellow River valley. These sites fill a gap in the distribution of Longshan sites in Northwestern Henan. The excavation at Xuecun in Xingyang revealed a large site spanning from the late Erlitou to the early Shang periods. The work is of significance in studying the structure of the settlement, the partition of functional areas, and the transition between Xia and Shang culture. From the Guandimiao site in Xingyang a well-preserved late Shang settlement was unearthed. This site can be divided into four distinct sections for habitation, pottery-making, sacrifice and burial. This is the first time an entire settlement from the Shang period has been uncovered. The excavation at Tanghu in Xinzheng revealed a large Peiligang cultural settlement. The characteristic housing organization, and drainage system reflect the advanced construction techniques of the Peiligang period.

Fourth, archaeological excavations and research are well combined. In the course of excavations, the conservation of various cultural relics has been enhanced through the use of modern scientific techniques to collect various samples. In particular, human and animal skeletal remains have been carefully examined and analyzed for sex, age, pathology and DNA. According to the national geographical information standard, ichnographies have been drawn for each site, establishing a good foundation for future surveys and conservation of cultural relics. For example, the Archaeology Department at Wuhan University has completely mapped a large Han tomb with nine chambers at Daguanzhuang in Huixian using three-dimensional techniques and closeup photography. Three-dimension models of archaeological objects have been created through digital mapping and virtual computer techniques. At Shandong University, over the course of the excavation at Xijincheng site in Boai, researchers have designed an environmental archaeological project incorporating paleophysiognomy, as well as study of fauna, flora, stone implements, pottery, and the site catchment area. This is an important attempt to develop multidisciplinary research.

The conservation work of the Water Diversion Project from South to North in Henan has overcome multiple hardships and run a glorious course. We have tried our best to explore new methods for the salvage conservation of cultural relics, to revitalize administrative thought and systems, foster professional teamwork, upgrade research through the construction of large-scale projects, and have produced extraordinary achievements. The excavations at Liuzhuang in Hebi, Gu'an in Anyang, Guandimiao in Xingyang, and Tanghu in Xinzheng were selected as among the "Top Ten New Archaeological Discoveries in China". The Conservation Office of Cultural Heritage for the Water Diversion from South to North, Henan Administration of Cultural Heritage was named by the State Administration of Cultural Heritage, as a "National Excellent Group in the Conservation of Cultural Heritage". The excavations at Liuzhuang in Hebi, Guandimiao in Xingyang, and Tanghu in Xinzheng were honored with the "Qualitative Award of National Field Archaeology".

The conservation of cultural relics in the Water Diversion Project from South to North in Henan province has been emphasized and supported by various leaders and the community at large. Zhang Siqing, vice-president of National Committee of CPPCC has visited the conservation work on cultural relics in the Water Diversion Project from South to North in Henan province. The leaders from the Conservation Office of Cultural Heritage for the Water Diversion from South to North, State Department and State Administration of Cultural Heritage have personally supervised archaeological fieldwork. The Henan Provincial Committee of the Chinese Communist Party, and Henan Provincial Government have held many meetings to examine and solve important problems regarding salvage conservation of cultural relics. A number of famous archaeologists, such as Huang Jinglue, Zhang Zhongpei, Xu Guangji, Zou Heng, and Li Boqian have visited archaeological sites many times and have provided help on significant academic questions and archaeological excavation techniques. The news media have paid considerable attention to the archaeological work that has been carried out in conjunction with the Project.

On the occasion of the upcoming third national "Cultural Heritage Day", Henan province will hold an exhibition of archaeological achievement for the Water Diversion Project from South to North, and will publish photographs in order to show the outstanding achievements of this project. It is our hope that this will begin to express our gratitude toward leaders and all of the society, as an open door for people to understand the salvage conservation work undertaken in conjunction with the Water Diversion Project from South to North.

安阳

釉陶莲花盘口瓶
(T1026M23:53)
东魏
高 27、口径 8.3 厘米

Glazed pottery vase with
dish-shaped mouth
designed in lotus
Eastern Wei
Height 27cm, rim diameter
8.3 cm

釉陶盘口壶(T1026M23:48)
东魏
高12.5、口径8.2、底径9.5
厘米

Glazed pottery pot with
dish-shaped mouth
Eastern Wei
Height 12.5 cm, rim diameter
8.2cm, base diameter 9.5cm

固岸墓地位于安阳县安丰乡固岸村和施家河村东部，面积约1000万平方米。南水北调总干渠在这里宽120米，从该墓地西部通过，占压墓地面积33.2万平方米。墓地以幸福渠为界分为两部分，渠南为发掘Ⅰ区，渠北为发掘Ⅱ区。Ⅰ区中部有一条南北向的灌溉渠，以此渠为界又分为东、西两部分。

从2005年9月1日开始发掘，发掘面积2.5万平方米，发掘面积占干渠占压墓地面积的7.5%。已经和正在发掘墓葬300多座，其中Ⅰ区151座，Ⅱ区188座。

据不完全统计，在这些墓葬中，战国时期的36座，秦汉时期的55座，魏晋时期的5座，十六国时期的3座，北朝时期的150余座（其中，北魏墓葬8座，东魏墓葬90多座，北齐墓葬60多座），隋唐时期的5座，清代的4座。其他正在发掘，时代尚待判定的墓葬100余座。

通过发掘，我们知道这里是一处以东魏、北齐时期为主的平民墓葬群。

这个墓地的家族性质明显，其墓葬分布排列有序，比较集中，相同级别的墓葬随葬品组合基本一样。

这一墓地的东魏、北齐墓葬具有明显的等级，根据目前所发掘的资料初步可以分为五个级别。

1. 级别最高，为带斜坡墓道的单室砖室墓。这类墓葬一般墓门南向，有砖雕仿木结构墓门，砖封门或石质墓门，石质墓门上雕刻有

釉陶莲花高足盘（T1026M23:55）
东魏
高8.5、口径12、底径9.5厘米

Glazed pottery dish with lotus shape and high foot
Eastern Wei
Height 8.5cm, rim diameter 12cm, base diameter 9.5cm

壁画，如Ⅱ区M24。随葬有成组的陶俑，甚至有石棺或石棺床。

2. 级别低于前者，为带天井、斜坡或梯形墓道的铲形洞室墓。这一类也为南向，墓室平面一般为长方形或梯形，棺木横放墓室的后部或竖放于墓室的西部。随葬有成组的陶俑或瓷器，多随葬有墓志砖，墓志砖摆放于墓道或天井内。有的有砖砌的棺床，个别的以围屏石座榻为葬具。

3. 级别低于前两者，为不带天井的斜坡墓道的铲形洞室墓。这一类也为南向，有仿木结构的砖雕墓门，墓室平面一般为长方形或梯形，有砖砌棺床，棺木横放于墓室的后部。随葬有成组的陶俑或瓷器，个别随葬有墓志砖，墓志砖摆放于墓道或天井内。没有明显的棺床。

4. 为斜坡墓道的刀形洞室墓。墓南向，墓室平面呈三角形或不规则梯形，墓室的东壁与墓道的东壁基本上成一直线，棺木沿西壁头向南摆放，没有棺床，为很浅的竖穴土坑墓。一般随葬有简单的陶器或瓷器数件。

5. 级别最低，为很浅的竖穴土坑墓。一般随葬有一件陶罐或铜钱，如M35。另外还有用瓦作为儿童葬具。

值得重视的是在此墓地发现的两座北周时期的墓葬，为该地区首次发现。

釉陶盆 （T1026M23:64）
东魏
高 5.3、口径 21.7、底径 16.6 厘米

Glazed pottery basin
Eastern Wei
Height 5.3cm, rim diameter 21.7 cm, base diameter 16.6cm

The Gu'an cemetery is located in Gu'an village and the eastern part of Shijiahe village of Anfeng town, Anyang county. It is 1000 ha. in area. In this area, the channel of the Water Diversion Project from South to North is 120 meters wide and passes through the western part of the cemetery, occupying 33.2 ha. of its total extent. The cemetery is divided into two parts by the Xingfu trench. To the south of the trench is section I of the excavation, and to the north is section II of the excavation. Section I is then divided into eastern and western parts by one irrigation channel, which passes through the center in south-north direction.

The excavation began in September 1, 2005. So far a total of 2.5 ha. has been uncovered. The excavated area accounts for 7.5% of the total occupied ceremonial area. The number of excavated graves is over 300, of which 151 belong to section I and 188 belong to section II. According to the preliminary statistics, there are 36 graves dating to the Warring States period, 55 to the Qin and Han periods, 5 to the Wei and Jin periods, 3 to the Sixteen States period, over 150 to the Northern Dynasty (of these, 8 to the Northern Wei, over 90 to the Eastern Wei, over 60 to the Northern Qi), 5 to the Sui and Tang periods, and 4 to the Qing period. More than 100 graves are still to be dated.

Based on what has been excavated so far, we know that most of the burial group dates to the

Eastern Wei and North Qi periods. This indicates a household cemetery with graves arranged in a particular order. The combination of grave goods is similar within the same class of graves.

There are obvious class differences among the Eastern Wei and Northern Qi graves. Using the present material, these graves can be generally sorted into five classes.

The first class includes single brick-chambered tombs with a sloped passageway. The tomb gates, generally facing south, include a carved brick gate that suggests a timber structure and stone gates with carved frescoes. The associated funeral objects consist of suites of pottery figurines,

a stone sarcophagus, and a stone platform for the coffin.

The second class includes a shovel-shaped cavity-chambered tomb with a dooryard, with a sloping or trapezoidal passage. The tomb gates also face south. The plan of the burial chamber is commonly rectangular or trapezoidal. The coffin was placed across the rear part of the chamber or along in the western part of the chamber. The funeral objects are suites of pottery figurines or porcelain. Most of the tombs were sealed with epitaph bricks, which were placed in the tomb passage or dooryard. Some have a brick platform for the coffin and a few used a stone couch with a

釉陶碗（T1026M23:56）
东魏
高 8.7、口径 12.2、底径 5 厘米

Glazed pottery bowl
Eastern Wei
Height 8.7cm, rim diameter 12.2cm,
base diameter 5cm

釉陶耳杯（T1026M23:61）
东魏
高8.3、口长径15.4、口短8.9、底长径6.6、
底短径4.7厘米

Glazed pottery cup
Eastern Wei
Height 8.3cm, long diameter of rim 15.4cm, short diameter of rim 8.9cm, long diameter of base 6.6cm, short diameter of base 4.7cm

round screen as burial furniture.

The third class consists of shovel-shaped cavity-chambered tombs without a dooryard. The tomb gates face south with a carved brick imitation timber structure. The plan of the burial chamber is commonly rectangular or trapezoidal, with a brick platform for the coffin. The coffin was placed across in the rear part of the chamber. A few tombs were sealed with epitaph bricks, which were placed in the tomb passage or dooryard. There is no platform for a coffin.

The fourth class consists of knife-shaped cavity-chambered tombs with a sloping passage. The tomb gates face south. The plan of the burial chamber is rectangular or an irregular trapezoid. The eastern wall of the burial chamber and the eastern wall of the tomb passage are generally in a straight line. The coffin was placed along the western wall, with the occupant of the tomb facing south. These are low shaft tombs without a platform for the coffin. The occupants were buried with several pottery or porcelain vessels.

The fifth class consists of low shaft tombs commonly including a ceramic jar or bronze coins.

It should be emphasized that two Northern Zhou tombs were found in the cemetery. It is the first time that tombs of this period have been found in the region.

釉陶熏炉（T1026M23:69）
东魏
通高 15.3、口径 3.8、底径 14 厘米

Glazed pottery incense burner
Eastern Wei
Height 15.3cm, rim diameter 3.8cm, base diameter 14cm

陶武士俑（T1026M23:50)
东魏
高 42.6 厘米

Pottery figurine of warrior
Eastern Wei
Height 42.6cm

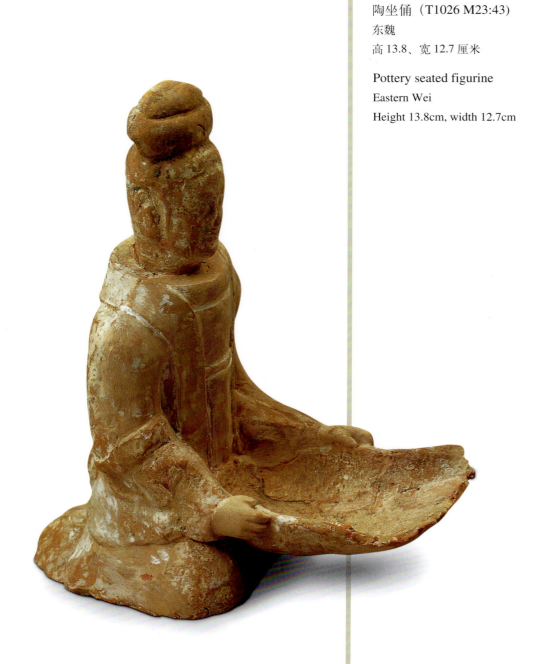

陶坐俑（T1026 M23:43）
东魏
高 13.8、宽 12.7 厘米

Pottery seated figurine
Eastern Wei
Height 13.8cm, width 12.7cm

陶狗（T1026M23:6）
东魏
高 7.6、长 16.5 厘米

Pottery dog
Eastern Wei
Height 7.6cm, length 16.5cm

陶狗（T1026M23:5）
东魏
高 4.7、长 11.5 厘米

Pottery dog
Eastern Wei
Height 4.7cm, length 11.5cm

陶羊（T1026M23:7）
东魏
高 10、长 14 厘米

Pottery sheep
Eastern Wei
Height 10cm, length 14cm

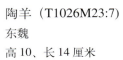

陶牛（M2:54）
北齐
高 19.8、长 27.2 厘米

Pottery cattle
Northern Qi
Height 19.8cm, length 27.2cm

围屏石榻局部
Part of stone couch with folding screen

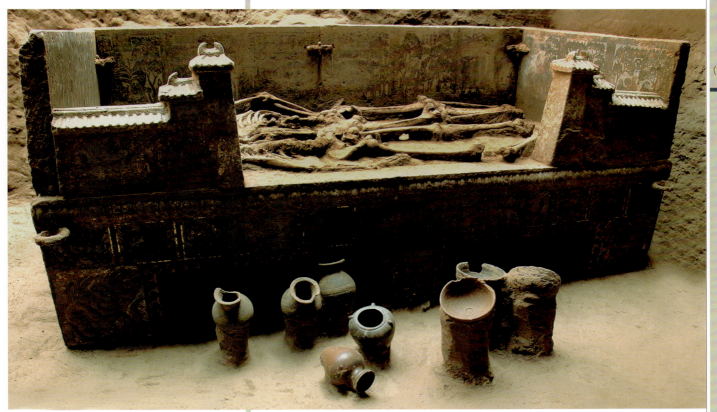

北齐墓围屏石榻（M57）
Stone couch with folding screen from Northern Qi tomb

釉陶罐（M2:13）
北齐
高 19、口径 7、底径 7 厘米

Glazed pottery jar
Northern Qi
Height 19cm, rim diameter 7cm, base
diameter 7cm

釉陶碗（M2:19）
北齐
高 9、口径 11、底径 5 厘米

Glazed pottery bowl
Northern Qi
Height 9cm, rim diameter 11cm,
base diameter 5cm

釉陶豆（M2:24）
北齐
高 13、口径 14、底径 11 厘米

Glazed pottery Dou
Northern Qi
Height 13cm, rim diameter 14cm,
base diameter 11cm

陶人面兽身镇墓兽
（M2:35）
北齐
高 32.8 厘米

Pottery animality patron in
tomb with human face and
animal body
Northern Qi
Height 32.8cm

陶狮面兽身镇墓兽
（M2:36）
北齐
高 34 厘米

Pottery animality patron in tomb
with lion face and animal body
Northern Qi
Height 34cm

陶武士俑（M2:53）
北齐
高 44 厘米

Pottery figurine of warrior
Northern Qi
Height 44cm

陶武士俑（M2:34）　　Pottery figurine of warrior
北齐　　　　　　　　Northern Qi
高 44 厘米　　　　　Height 44cm

陶文吏俑（M2:37）
北齐
高 24.2 厘米

Pottery figurine of civil official
Northern Qi
Height 24.2cm

陶文吏俑（M2:27）　　Pottery figurine of civil official
北齐　　Northern Qi
高 24 厘米　　Height 24cm

陶文吏俑（M2:25）
北齐
通高 24.3 厘米

Pottery figurine of
civil official
Northern Qi
Height 24.3cm

陶武吏俑（M2:44）
北齐
通高 24.2 厘米

Pottery figurine of
martial official
Northern Qi
Height 24.2cm

陶武吏俑（M2:52）
北齐
通高 25.6 厘米

Pottery figurine of
martial official
Northern Qi
Height 25.6cm

陶武吏俑（M2:42）
北齐
通高 25.6 厘米

Pottery figurine of
martial official
Northern Qi
Height 25.6cm

陶武吏俑（M2:48）
北齐
通高 24.2 厘米

Pottery figurine of
martial official
Northern Qi
Height 24.2cm

陶武吏俑（M2:33）
北齐
通高 24.8 厘米

Pottery figurine of
martial official
Northern Qi
Height 24.8cm

陶侍俑（M2:31）
北齐
通高 23.7 厘米

Pottery figurine of servant
Northern Qi
Height 23.7cm

陶侍俑（M2:46)
北齐
通高 23.7 厘米

Pottery figurine of servant
Northern Qi
Height 23.7cm

陶尖顶风帽俑（M2:26）
北齐
高 22.7 厘米

Pottery figurine with capuche
Northern Qi
Height 22.7cm

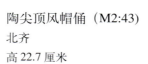

陶尖顶风帽俑（M2:43）
北齐
高 22.7 厘米

Pottery figurine with capuche
Northern Qi
Height 22.7cm

陶圆平顶风帽俑（M2:39）
北齐
高 24 厘米

Pottery figurine with
round-flatted crest wind hat
Northern Qi
Height 24cm

陶圆平顶风帽俑（M2:51）
北齐
高 24 厘米

Pottery figurine with round-
flatted crest wind hat
Northern Qi
Height 24cm

郭里墓地
Guoli cemetery

　　郭里墓地位于安阳市龙安区东风乡郭里村东北，处于太行山东麓山前丘陵与平原交界地区。20世纪70年代，安阳市博物馆曾在墓地东部发掘汉代墓葬60余座，出土陶罐、仓、灶、井等器物。2005年8~9月，中国社会科学院考古研究所、安阳市文物工作队对该墓地进行了发掘，共发掘古墓葬49座。其中汉墓26座，宋墓23座。出土铜、铁、陶（包括绿釉陶器）、瓷器及铜钱等器物300余件。

　　汉墓均为砖室墓，可分为双室墓和单室墓两大类。双室墓分为双室带双耳室墓、双室带单耳室墓、双室无耳室墓三种。单室墓分为单室带单耳室墓和单室无耳室墓两种。出土的器物主要为陶器，主要有罐、壶、仓、灶、井、奁、盘、盆及长方形盒。另外还有铜镜、带钩和各类铜钱等。其中出土的5件绿釉陶壶、4件陶羊尊、2件鹿尊，造型奇特，为汉墓所不多见，具有很高的研究价值。出土的车马出行图案铜镜，极为罕见，可谓汉代铜镜中的精品。

　　宋墓可分为砖室墓、土洞墓和土坑墓三种。在砖室墓中发现有砖雕格扇门、窗、桌、凳、条几、灯架等。宋墓中的随葬品比较单一，大多只随葬1件瓷罐，多者也仅有3件瓷器和一些铜钱。

　　通过郭里墓地的发掘，对安阳地区汉代砖室墓的形制、砌筑方式、随葬习俗等有了进一步的认识。郭里的宋代小型砖室墓，砌筑方法独特，小巧精致，砖雕图案丰富、逼真，是安阳宋墓的典型代表。

陶鹿尊（M61:4）   Pottery deer-shaped Zun

汉   Han

高 22.3、长 39.2 厘米   Height 22.3cm, length 39.2cm

陶羊尊（M58:2）　　Pottery sheep-shaped Zun
汉　　　　　　　　Han
高 20.8、长 38.5 厘米　Height 20.8 cm, length 38.5cm

The cemetery is located in north-eastern Guoli village, Dongfeng town, Longan district of Anyang city. Anyang Museum excavated more than 60 Han tombs in the eastern part of the cemetery in 1970s, and unearthed pottery jars, storehouses, stoves, and wells. From August to September of 2005, the Institute of Archaeology, Chinese Academy of Social Sciences, and Anyang Munici-pal Team of Cultural Heritage exca-vated the cemetery. They uncovered 49 tombs, of which there are 26 Han tombs and 23 Song tombs, and col-lected more than 300 artifacts involved in bronze, iron, pottery (including green glazed pottery), porcelain and coins.

All of the Han tombs are brick-chambered tombs, which can be divided into double chamber and single chamber categories. The double chamber tombs can be classified into double chamber with double side chamber, double chamber with single side chamber, and double chamber without side chamber. The single chamber tombs include single chamber with a single side chamber and single chamber without a side chamber. Most of the unearthed artifacts are pottery vessels including jars, pots, storehouses, stoves, wells, Lian, dishes, basins and rectangular cases. Moreover, there are bronze mirrors, belt hooks and various bronze coins. Of these, five green glazed pottery pots, four pottery sheep-shaped Zun, and two deer-shaped Zun are rare due to their peculiar shapes. The unearthed bronze mirror with the pattern of procession scene of chariot and horse is an article of fine quality in Han bronze mirrors.

The Song tombs can be divided into brick-chambered, cavity-chambered and shaft tombs. Brick-carved doors with lattice pattern, windows, tables, benches, bars, and lamp frames were found in brick-chambered tombs. The funeral objects from the Song tombs are relatively simple. Most of the tombs contained one porcelain jar only, and very few tombs included three porcelain vessels and some bronze coins.

The excavation at Guoli provides the information about the structure, building mode, and burial custom of Han brick-chambered tombs in Anyang region. The Song tombs are small brick-chambered tombs with realistic brick-carved patterns and were built with an unusual technique. They represent the Song tombs in Anyang.

鹤壁

◎ 刘庄遗址

◎ 关庄墓地

刘庄遗址

Liuzhuang site

刘庄遗址位于鹤壁市淇滨区大赉店镇刘庄村，为市级文物保护单位。2005年6月至2006年底，河南省文物考古研究所同鹤壁市文物工作队，并邀请郑州大学、山东大学、河南大学考古系师生40余人组成考古队对刘庄遗址进行

了考古发掘，发掘面积15000平方米，取得了重要考古收获。

遗址下层为仰韶时代大司空类型文化遗存，发现有房址、窖穴、灰坑、灰沟、灶坑、陶片铺垫遗迹等。出土遗物主要为陶器、石器、鹿角等。陶器有罐、瓮、钵、

陶罐（H79:1）
新石器时代（仰韶文化）
高30.5、口径17.8、
底径10.5厘米

Pottery jar
Neolithic Age (Yangshao culture)
Height 30.5cm, rim diameter 17.8cm,
base diameter 10.5cm

彩陶钵（H724:1）
新石器时代（仰韶文化）
高 10.2、口径 22、底径 8 厘米

Painted pottery bowl
Neolithic Age (Yangshao culture)
Height 10.2cm, rim diameter 22cm,
base diameter 8cm

陶钵（T4742 灰堆Ⅱ:12）
新石器时代（仰韶文化）
高 9、口径 21.6、底径 10.5 厘米

Pottery bowl
Neolithic Age (Yangshao culture)
Height 9cm, rim diameter 21.6cm,
base diameter 10.5cm

陶钵（T4741 灰堆Ⅱ:18）
新石器时代（仰韶文化）
高 7.2、口径 18、底径 7.5 厘米

Pottery bowl
Neolithic Age (Yangshao culture)
Height 7.2cm, rim diameter 18cm,
base diameter 7.5cm

碗、盆、器盖等，彩陶器尤为精美。石器有铲、斧、凿、锛、钻头、球等。遗址上层为先商文化墓地，共发掘墓葬 300 多座。这一时期发现如此规模的先商文化墓地，在黄河下游地区无论是夏文化，还是先商文化、东夷文化均为第一次发现，极具历史、考古价值。

先商文化墓地的发现为先商文化的发掘研究填补了一项空白，是该研究领域的一项重大学术突破。该墓地的揭露将对先商文化墓葬制度、人种族属、社会结构、商人渊源、夷夏商关系等重要学术问题的研究起到巨大的推进作用。

陶折腹盆 （H291:1）
新石器时代（仰韶文化）
高8.4、口径16.6、底径7.5厘米

Pottery belly-folded basin
Neolithic Age (Yangshao culture)
Height 8.4cm, rim diameter 16.6cm, base diameter 7.5cm

彩陶钵 （H724:2）
新石器时代（仰韶文化）
高7、口径16.5、底径6.5厘米

Painted pottery bowl
Neolithic Age (Yangshao culture)
Height 7cm, rim diameter 16.5cm, base diameter 6.5cm

Liuzhuang site is located in Liuzhuang village, Dalaidian town, Qibin district of Hebi city. It is one of the major historical and cultural monuments under municipal protection. From June of 2005 to the end of 2006, a combined archaeological team with more than 40 people from Henan Provincial Institute of Cultural Relics and Archaeology, Hebi Municipal Team of Cultural Heritage, Zhengzhou University, Shandong University, and Henan University excavated the Liuzhuang site. A total of 1.5 ha. of the site was uncovered. This excavation made a number of important achievements.

The lower layer of this site is the typical Dasikong remains of the Yangshao culture. The excavation revealed house foundations, storages, pits, ash ditches, stove pits, and features paved with ceramic sherds. A large number of archaeological objects, mainly including pottery vessels, stone tools, and deer antlers,

陶鬲 （M256:1）
先商
高 19.6、口径 13.5 厘米

Pottery Li
Pre-shang
Height 19.6cm, rim diameter
13.5cm

was also collected. The pottery vessels included jars, urns, bowls, basins covers, and so on. Painted pottery vessels are quite beautiful. Stone implements included shovels, axes, chisels, adzes, aiguilles, and balls.

The upper layer of the site is a Pre-shang cemetery from which over 300 tombs were uncovered. It is for the first time we find such a large Pre-shang cemetery in the lower Yellow River valley, including the contemporaneous Xia culture, or the Pre-shang and Dongyi cultures. The discovery of this cemetery fills up the gap in our understanding of the Pre-shang culture, and promotes the research on the burial system, ethnic groups, social structure, the origin of Shang people, and the relationship between Yi, Xia, and Shang.

陶鼎（M218:3）
先商
高19、口径24、底径16厘米

Pottery Ding tripod
Pre-shang
Height 19cm, rim diameter 24cm, base
diameter 16cm

陶鬲（M218:2）
先商
高18、口径14.5厘米

Pottery Li
Pre-shang
Height 18cm, rim diameter 14.5cm

陶鬲 （M236:1）

先商

高 16.5、口径 13.3 厘米

Pottery Li

Pre-shang

Height 16.5cm, rim diameter
13.3cm

陶簋 （M4:2）

先商

高 16.3、口径 24、
圈足径 15.7 厘米

Pottery Gui

Pre-shang

Height 16.3cm, rim diameter 24cm,
circular base diameter 15.7cm

陶盘（M218:1）

先商

高 18.3、口径 19.5、圈足径 19.5 厘米

Pottery dish

Pre-shang

Height 18.3cm, rim diameter 19.5cm,

circular base diameter 19.5cm

陶罐（M4:1）
先商
高 11、口径 10.5、
底径 6.8 厘米

Pottery jar

Pre-shang

Height 11cm, rim diameter
10.5cm, base diameter 6.8cm

陶豆（M218:4）
先商
高 16.1、口径 18、
底径 10.5 厘米

Pottery Dou

Pre-Shang

Height 16.1cm, rim diameter
18cm, base diameter 10.5cm

陶盘（M236:4）
先商
高 16.6、口径 16.5、
圈足径 16.5 厘米

Pottery dish
Pre-shang
Height 16.6cm, rim diameter 16.5cm,
circular base diameter 16.5cm

石钺（M35:1）
先商
高 19.5、口径 13.5、孔径 2 厘米

Stone Yue

Pre-shang

Height 19.5cm, orifice diameter 13.5cm, hole diameter 2cm

关庄墓地
Guanzhuang cemetery

关庄墓地位于鹤壁市淇县铁西区关庄村西，墓地系太行山山前地带，西距金牛岭3公里，地势由西北向东南倾斜。南水北调干渠从墓地的中部穿过，干渠占压墓地面积50000平方米。

2006年8~12月，河南省文物考古研究所、濮阳市文物保护管理所、淇县文物保护管理所对墓地进行勘探发掘，实际发掘面积5700平方米，清理汉代墓葬40座，清代墓4座，汉代沟3条达190多米，汉代

水井1口。出土铜、铁、陶、石、金银首饰等一批重要文物。

汉代墓葬多为砖室墓，坐西朝东，少数坐南朝北，且大多被盗掘。洞室墓道有竖井式、斜坡式和阶梯式三种，按墓室结构可分为单室墓、单室单耳室墓、单室双耳室墓、双室单耳室墓。

双室墓的前室多为方形圆角穹窿顶砖室，为叠涩砌法；后室分为砖室或洞室。凡带有弯曲斜坡墓道的砖室墓，一般墓道窄长，有

陶盒（M18:17）　汉　通高15.3、长27.4、宽15厘米
Pottery case　Han　Height 15.3cm, length 27.4cm, width 15cm

陶灶（M34 东室）　汉　高 21、长 39、宽 24 厘米
Pottery stove　Han　Height 21cm, length 39cm, width 24cm

封门石或封门砖，前甬道前室，后甬道后室，左右各有两耳室，规模较大结构复杂，建造规整，但被盗严重，只有少量的陶片出土。从少量未被盗的小型砖室墓看（如M15 随葬品陶器组合完整，随葬陶器大陶壶 6 件，小陶壶 3 件，陶瓮 1 件，陶罐 2 件，陶仓 3 件，陶灶 1 件，铁剑 1 件，铁刀 1 件，五铢钱等），该墓地时代为西汉至东汉晚期。

清代墓葬为土坑墓，其中 M9 为清康熙四十三年（1704 年）西安府守备孙振夫妇合葬墓，出土墓志记载孙振为淇县北阳镇南阳人，与

《淇县县志》记载相吻合。该墓出土金质首饰造型优美，制作精细，纹饰饱满瑰丽，是难得的艺术珍品。

勘探发掘表明关庄墓地与临近大马庄、黄庄墓地同属西汉晚期至东汉晚期的大型墓群，墓群年代、墓葬形制、器物组合明确，陶器制作工艺精致，种类繁多，出土有少量釉陶器器盖。墓群分布密集、排列有序。虽然墓葬被盗，出土物不甚丰富，但是反映了淇县墓地的基本形制，为研究鹤壁地区汉代墓葬形制的演变及这一时期的政治、经济、文化等提供了重要的考古资料。

金首饰（M9:1）
清
直径 12.8 厘米

Golden ornament
Qing
Diameter 12.8cm

金耳坠（M9:2）
清
长 4.3 厘米

Golden earbob
Qing
Length 4.3cm

铜冠帽饰（M9:3）
清
高 9.8 厘米

Copper headgear ornament
Qing
Height 9.8cm

铜簪花（M9:4）
清
长 7.9 厘米

Copper hairpin
Qing
Length 7.9cm

新乡

◎ 王门 墓地
◎ 大司马墓地
◎ 毡匠屯墓地
◎ 大官庄墓地

王门墓地
Wangmen cemetery

王门墓地位于新乡市凤泉区潞王坟乡王门村北，北依太行山余脉凤凰山，系凤凰山向南延伸的岗坡地带，地势略高。墓葬分布密集，东北临明代潞简王墓。

2006年8~12月，河南省文物考古研究所、新乡市文物工作队对墓地进行了勘探发掘。发掘面积4000平方米，发掘战国墓3座，汉墓59座，汉代陶窑1座，宋墓1座，清墓1座，不明年代墓2座。出土铜、铁、琉璃、陶、瓷器等文物700余件。

战国墓葬均为长方形竖穴土坑墓，墓主均为单人一次屈肢葬。出土器物均为陶器，陶器基本组合为鼎、豆、壶、匜。

汉代墓葬有土洞墓和砖室墓。土洞墓墓道为竖穴短墓道。砖室墓多为单室券顶，墓壁为单砖错缝平砌，墓道为斜坡长墓道。除M28未被盗扰外，余皆被盗扰。M28出土器物有陶罐、壶、仓、碗、盘、四足炉、盒、奁、猪

陶鼎（M28:30）
汉
高 16.8、口径 9.8 厘米

Pottery Ding tripod
Han
Height 16.8cm, rim diameter
9.8cm

陶仓（M28:11）
汉
通高 31.5、口径 9.4 厘米
Pottery storage container
Han
Height 31.5cm, rim diameter 9.4cm

圈、灶、井、耳杯、器盖及铁矛、剑、削刀，铜带钩、五铢钱、镏金铜盆，琉璃蝉、鼻塞等。其中镏金铜盆保存较好，为新乡地区汉墓所仅见。M60 发现有盖尸用的苇席痕迹，这在新乡地区也是首次发现，为了解汉代葬俗提供了新的资料。

汉代陶窑为半地穴式，平面为瓶胆状，由操作坑、火门、火膛、窑床、烟道（3 个）组成。窑顶虽然坍塌，但可看出是用土坯券顶，保存较好，为研究汉代的制陶技术提供了实物资料。

王门墓地是一处西汉晚期至东汉时期的大型墓群，墓葬分布密集，排列有序，墓葬年代、形制、器物组合明确，为研究新乡地区汉代的埋葬习俗、埋葬制度、墓葬形制的演变及这一时期的政治、经济、文化等提供了丰富的考古资料。

陶井（M5:1）
汉
高 24.5 厘米

Pottery well
Han
Height 24.5cm

The Wangmen cemetery is located in the northern Wangmen village, Luwangfen town, district of Xinxiang city. To the north, it is the Fenghuang Mountain, part of the Taihang Mountain. The topography of the cemetery is elevated, and the burials are densely distributed.

Henan Provincial Institute of Cultural Relics and Archaeology and Xinxiang Municipal Team of Archaeology excavated the cemetery from August to December of 2006. The excavation area is 0.4 ha. The team uncovered 3 Warring States tombs, 59 Han tombs, one Han pottery kiln, one Song tomb, one Qing tomb, and 2 tombs with unknown dates. The team also recovered more than 700 bronze, iron, colored glaze, pottery, and porcelain artifacts.

All Warring States tombs are

陶猪 （M31:23）
汉
大猪长 10.04、宽 5.7 厘米
小猪长 5.1、宽 1.7 厘米

Pottery pigs
Han
Length 10.04cm, width 5.7cm
Length 5.1cm, width 1.7cm

rectangular shaft tombs, and always include a single flexed burial. All funeral objects are pottery vessels with basic combination of Ding tripod, Dou, and pot.

Han tombs include cavity-chambered and brick-chambered tombs. The cavity-chambered tombs are vertical pits and short passages. The brick-chambered tombs are mostly single-chambered tombs with arch-shaped roof, and possess a slope and long passage. All of the tombs except M28 were looted. The funeral objects from M28 included a ceramic jar, a pot, a storage, a bowl, a dish, a furnace with four feet, a box, a Lian, a sty, a stove, a well, a cup, and a lid, an iron spear, a sword, as well as a knife, a bronze

belt hook, a Wuzhu coin, and a basin with gold-plating, a colored-glaze cicada, and a nose stopper. Of these, the bronze basin with gold-plating is well-preserved and only seen in Han tombs in Xinxiang region. The mark of reed mat was found for the first time in M60 in Xinxiang region.

Wangmen cemetery is a large cemetery dating to the late Western Han to Eastern Han periods. The burials were densely arranged. It is clear in date, form, and combination of funeral objects. The cemetery provides rich materials for investigating the burial customs, the change of burial form, as well as of politics, economy, and culture in Xinxinag region in the Han Dynasty.

陶灶（M28:9）

汉

通高 26.1、长 32.3、宽 21 厘米

Pottery stove

Han

Height 26.1cm, length 32.3cm, width 21cm

陶猪圈（M31:23）

汉

高 26、长 33.2、宽 22.5 厘米

Pottery sty

Han

Height 26cm, length 33.2cm, width 22.5cm

大司马墓地

Dasima cemetery

大司马墓地位于新乡卫辉市唐庄镇大司马村村北，总面积约70万平方米，市级文物保护单位。2006年6~10月，四川大学考古学系对其进行了考古发掘，发掘面积3000平方米，清理墓葬28座，其中汉墓1座，西晋墓4座，唐墓1座，宋墓3座，明清墓17座。另有2座带长斜坡墓道的土洞墓，因部队光缆通过墓室，仅发掘了墓道部分，墓室情况不详。共出土文物近400件。

晋墓中三墓并列，皆为前带长斜坡墓道之土洞墓，坐北朝南，多以大型空心砖封砌墓门，墓室与墓道之间以短甬道相接。随葬品组合完整，出有镇墓兽、武士俑、男女立俑、牛车，罐、盘、樽、碗、碟、耳杯、长方形多子盒、灶、井、磨、碓、仓，鸡、狗，另有铜镜、弩机、五铢钱等。三座墓葬排列有序，墓室构筑方式相同，随葬器物的种类、组合和风格特点亦很相似，推测应为同一时代相差

陶镇墓兽(M21:37)　西晋　高20、长33.3厘米
Pottery animality patron in tomb　Western Jin　Height 20cm, length 33.3cm

不远的西晋家族墓地。

　　唐墓为长方形单室土洞墓，坐北朝南，由墓道、天井、甬道、墓室四部分组成。石门位于甬道南端，由门楣、立颊、门下坎、门扇、石狮等青石构件组成。墓室和甬道带红、黑、绿等彩绘。出土墓志两方，四神石刻1套，石灯6件，还有青瓷碗、器盖等。陶俑经修复较完整的有近40件，有文吏俑、骑马俑、立俑等，多施彩绘，个别描金。墓主为隋代"使持节柱国西河郡开国公"乞扶令和夫人郁久闾氏。墓志中有若干内容不见于《北史》、《隋书》等正史文献记载。

　　两汉、晋唐和宋明清等各个不同时段的墓葬在大司马墓地均有发现，证明该墓地的延续时间很长。此次将汉墓的附属建筑较为完整地揭露出来，是本次发掘的一大收获。晋、唐墓葬规模较大、形制清楚、出土器物丰富，在整个豫东北地区都是不多见的。明清墓葬中出土的朱书板瓦，则为研究明清时期道教对墓葬制度的影响提供了新的实物史料。

陶立俑（M20:21）　　Pottery standing figurine
西晋　　　　　　　　Western Jin
高 22.5 厘米　　　　Height 22.5cm

The Dasima cemetery is located in the north of Dasima village, Tangzhuang town, Weihui city, Xinxiang. The total area of the cemetery is about 70 ha. Archaeology Department of Sichuan University conducted the excavation from June to October of 2006, and revealed 28 tombs within the area of 3000 square meters. These tombs include one Han tomb, 4 Western Jin tombs, one Tang tomb, 3 Song tomb, 17 Ming and Qing tombs, as well as other two disturbed tombs. About 400 objects were recovered from these tombs.

Among the Western Jin tombs, three were arranged in parallel, facing south. All of them are cavity-chambered tombs with long and sloping passages. Large air bricks were used to close tomb gates. The composition of funeral objects is complete. The funeral objects are zoomorphic patrons of tomb, a figurine of warrior, male and female standing figurines, a cattle cart, a jar, a dish, a Zun, a bowl, a small dish, a cup, a rectangular multi-lattice box, a stove, a well, a mill, a pestle, a storage, a chicken, a dog, a bronze mirror, a Nuji, a Wuzhu coin, and so on. Based on the information mentioned above, this was likely a family cemetery of the Western Jin Dynasty.

The Tang tomb is a single-chambered cavity tomb composed of a passage, a dooryard, a corridor and a chamber. Epitaphs, carved stones, stone lamps, celadon bowls, lids, and pottery figurines were recovered from the tomb. The figurines include a civil official, a harnessed horse, and some standing figurines. Most of the pottery figurines were painted with colors and a few were drawn on with gold. The occupant of the tombs is Qifuling, a high official in the Sui Dynasty, and his wife Yujiulushi. Some information of the epitaph was not recorded in the official historical documents, Beishi, Suishu.

The finding of the Western Han,

陶立俑（M19:12）　　　Pottery standing figurine
西晋　　　　　　　　　 Western Jin
高 22.5 厘米　　　　　　 Height 22.5cm

陶立俑（M19:20）　　　Pottery standing figurine
西晋　　　　　　　　　 Western Jin
高 36.2 厘米　　　　　　 Height 36.2cm

Eastern Han, Jin, Tang, Song, Ming and Qing tombs at the Dasima cemetery indicates that this cemetery lasted a long time. The complete excavation of the Han tomb and its affiliated buildings is one of the important achievements for this fieldwork. The Jin and Tang tombs are large in size, clear in form and rich in offering object. It is rare in the whole northeastern Henan. The unearthed flat tiles with red writing from Ming and Qing tombs provide new materials for investigating the burial system influenced by Taoism in the Ming and Qing Dynasties.

陶俑组合(M23)　唐　高 20.8~26.1 厘米
Pottery figurines　Tang　Heights 20.8~26.1cm

陶文吏俑（M16:38）
唐
高 70 厘米

Pottery figurine of civil official
Tang
Height 70cm

陶镇墓兽（M16:64）　　　　Pottery animality patron in tomb
唐　　　　　　　　　　　　Tang
高 34.1 厘米　　　　　　　Height 34.1cm

陶马（M16:44）
唐
高 30.7、长 30、宽 20.8 厘米

Pottery horse
Tang
Height 30.7cm, length 30cm, width 20.8cm

陶多子盒（M21:29）
西晋
高 7.5、长 32.6、宽 20 厘米

Pottery multi-lattice case
Western Jin
Height 7.5cm, length 32.6cm, width 20cm

铜镜（M20:30）
西晋
直径 9、厚 0.3 厘米

Bronze mirror
Western Jin
Diameter 9cm, depth 0.3cm

陶骑马俑组合(M23)

唐

高 27.1~29.5 厘米

Pottery figurines of cavalrymen

Tang

Heights 27.1-29.5cm

毡匠屯墓地

Zhanjiangtun cemetery

陶鸭（M24:35）　汉　高20.5、长19.6厘米　　　Pottery duck　Han　Height 20.5cm, length 19.6cm

毡匠屯墓地位于辉县市路固村与毡匠屯村范围内。2006年6月，重庆市文物考古研究所对该墓地进行了发掘，发掘面积4000余平方米。共清理各类遗迹91处，出土遗物约400件。遗迹以墓葬为主，共55座，包括17座汉代墓葬，8座唐代墓葬，27座宋代墓葬和3座清代墓葬，另外还有灰坑31座、水井2口，道路1条，沟2条等其他遗迹。

汉代墓葬可分为砖室墓和土洞墓两大类。唐代墓葬皆是带阶梯竖井式墓道的小型单室土洞墓。

个别墓葬用砖棺床，其余各墓都发现了保存完好的随葬品。出土有陶罐、陶瓶、漆盒（及其上的铁扣）、铁剪、铜镜、瓷盏、铁发饰、铜钱、蚌饰、木梳等器物。

宋代墓葬皆为带竖井式墓道的小型土洞墓。墓内出土随葬品种类包括铜、铁、陶、瓷、银等，器物有铜簪、瓷盏、瓷碗、瓷罐、陶盆、铁铺首、银耳饰及铜钱等。

本次发掘为该地区汉代以来的墓葬特点和发展规律以及各时期生产生活内容的研究提供了重要考古资料。

陶狗（M38:6）
汉
高23、长31、宽10.4厘米

Pottery dog
Han
Height 23cm, length 31cm, width 10.4cm

陶井（M54:25）
汉
高 45.1、底径 23 厘米

Pottery well
Han
Height 45.1cm, base diameter
23cm

瓷碗（M22:1）
宋
高 3.9、口径 8.4、
底径 3.2 厘米

Porcelain bowl
Song
Height 3.9cm, rim diameter 8.4cm,
base diameter 3.2cm

瓷枕（M14:1）
宋
高 7.9、长 22.2、宽 18.5 厘米

Porcelain pillow
Song
Height 7.9cm, length 22.2cm,
width 18.5cm

The Zhanjiangtun cemetery is located in the area of Lugu village and Zhanjiangtun village. Chunqing Municipal Institute of Cultural Relics and Archaeology excavated the cemetery in June of 2006. More than 4000 square meters were excavated, 91 features were uncovered and about 400 artifacts were collected. The excavation uncovered 55 tombs, including 17 Han tombs, 8 Tang tombs, 27 Song tombs and 3 Qing tombs.

The Han tombs can be divided into two categories, brick-chambered and cavity-chambered tombs. The Tang tombs are all small single-chambered cavity tombs with step-vertical passage. Most of the un-earthed tombs included well-preserved offering objects, including pottery jars, vases, lacquer boxes, iron scissors, bronze mirrors, porcelain cups, iron hair decorations, bronze coins, shell decorations, and wooden combs.

All Song tombs were small cavity-chambered tombs with a vertical passage. The offerings include bronze, iron, pottery, porcelain, and silver objects. Among the recovered artifacts were bronze hairpins, porcelain cups, bowls and jars, pottery basins, iron gilt escutcheons silver ear decorations, and coins. This excavation provides important materials for investigating the burial characteristics and the production and subsistence in the region after the Han Dynasty.

大官庄墓地
Daguanzhuang cemetery

大官庄墓地位于辉县市百泉镇大官庄村东北部，2006年7月22日，武汉大学历史学院科技考古研究中心开始对大官庄墓群进行抢救性考古发掘。实际发掘面积近3200平方米，共清理陶窑1座，汉墓18座，唐墓4座，宋墓6座，其他墓葬10座，环壕1条。出土陶、瓷、玉、石和金属类文物600余件。

陶窑时代属东汉中晚期，可分工作坑、水井、工作面和窑室4部分。这种工作坑、水井和窑室一体化的陶窑尚属少见。

汉墓形制包括土坑墓、土洞墓、单券砖室墓以及由穹窿顶和券顶组成的多室墓等，几乎包括了已发现东汉墓的全部形制。除两座被盗，其他墓葬都保存完好，这在河南东汉墓的考古发掘中尚属少见。这批东汉墓的共同特点是：布局规整（所有墓葬均在环壕

铜镜（M8:2） 汉 直径15.5厘米
Bronze mirror Han Diameter 15.5cm

铜镜（M14:15） 汉 直径14.4厘米
Bronze mirror　Han　Diameter 14.4cm

以北），墓道方向一致（均位于墓室东部）。典型墓葬有单一竖穴土坑墓、土坑竖穴洞室墓、单一土坑单券墓、土坑多券墓、单一土坑穹窿顶墓、穹窿顶券顶多室墓等。其中M2为多室式土坑砖室墓，全墓由长斜坡墓道和9个砖室组成，其中券顶砖室5个，穹窿顶砖室4个。墓道位于墓室东部，长18米，上口宽70～150厘米。紧接墓道依次为单体券顶墓室（前室）、穹窿顶墓室（前堂）、穹窿顶墓室（后厅）、单体券顶墓室（后室），四者与墓道构成M2的中轴线。在前堂左右各有一单体穹窿顶和券顶墓室，在后厅左侧为一单体穹窿顶墓室，

右侧为两个并排的券顶墓室。该墓虽遭两次盗掘，但墓葬整体结构保存完好。在墓室内共清理人骨架11具，各类文物100余件。

环壕1条，位于墓地的中南部，东西横跨墓地的中区和西区。沟内出土物有东汉铜箭镞、铜戈、铜镜残片，还有陶豆、罐、砖、瓦残片等。

现有发掘收获表明，大官庄墓地是一处十分重要的汉代墓地，从发现的陶窑、环壕等遗迹来看，该墓地具备了从整体规划到具体建设实施的墓地建设理念，对该墓地的系统发掘将有助于解决汉代（尤其是东汉）墓葬制度中的许多问题。

The Daguanzhuang cemetery is located in the northeast of Daguanzhuang village, Baiquan town in Weihui city. The Research Center for Archaeological Sciences of History School at Wuhan University excavated the cemetery in the second half of 2006. The excavation area is 3200 square meters. The excavation revealed one pottery kiln, 18 Han tombs, 4 Tang tombs, 6 Song tombs, 10 other periods of tombs, and one ditch, and collected more than 600 objects including pottery, porcelain, jade, stone and metal categories.

The pottery kiln dating to the mid-late Eastern Han is composed of the working pit, well, working position and kiln chamber. The kind of pottery kiln that incorporates the working pit, well and kiln chamber is uncommonly observed. This discovery provides the important information for investigating the cemetery layout, production of raw materials and construction procedure in the Eastern Han.

The Han tombs can be divided into shaft tomb, cavity-chambered tomb, brick-chambered tomb and multi-chambered tombs, nearly involved in all the found forms of Eastern Han tombs. Except for two tombs that were looted, the rest tombs were well preserved. The cemetery has common characteristics, the regular layout and the same direction for tomb passage. M2 is a brick-chambered with multi-chambers. It is composed of a long and slope passage and nine brick-chambers including five arch-roofed chambers and four vault chambers. The tomb passage is located in the eastern part of the tomb with 18m long and 70-150cm wide. The chambers along from the passage are one arch-roofed chamber (atria), two vault chambers (antechamber and rear hall), and one arch-roofed chamber (rear chamber). The four chambers and the passage constitute the axis of M2. There are one vault chamber and one arch-roofed chamber in right and left sides of the antechamber. To the left side of rear hall is one vault chamber and to the right side are two arch-roofed chambers side by side. Although the tomb was looted, the whole structure

银镯（M14:8、10） Sliver bracelets
北宋 Northern Song
长径 6.2~6.8、短径 4.7~5.4 厘米 Long diameters 6.2-6.8cm, short diameters 4.7-5.4cm

of the tomb is well preserved. Eleven human skeletons and over 100 artifacts were recovered form the chambers.

The ditch is located in the central-south of the cemetery and crosses the central and western areas of the cemetery in west-east direction. Bronze arrows, daggers and mirror pieces, as well as pottery Dou, jars, bricks, and tiles dating to the Eastern Han were recovered the ditch.

The excavation indicates that the Daguanzhuang cemetery is an important Han cemetery. The discovery of the pottery kiln and ditch suggests that the cemetery was embedded in a construction idea from the whole design to the construction. The systematic excavation at the cemetery will contribute to solve many issues about the burial system in the Han Dynasty (especially Eastern Han).

焦作

◎ 聩城寨墓群

◎ 徐堡遗址

◎ 聂村墓地

◎ 山后墓地

◎ 苏王墓地

◎ 西金城遗址

聭城寨墓地

Kuichengzhai cemetery

聭城寨墓地位于焦作市马村区九里山乡聭城寨村西北,面积42万余平方米,市级文物保护单位。2006年5~12月,河南省文物考古研究所对聭城寨墓地进行了勘探和发掘工作,发掘面积3700平方米,清理战国、汉代、清代墓葬33座,灰坑32个,灰沟2条,出土一批战国、汉代和仰韶文化时期的重要文物。

战国墓葬均为长方形竖穴土坑墓,葬式有仰身屈肢、俯身屈肢、侧身屈肢3种。随葬陶器的基本组合为鼎、豆、壶,为战国中小型墓葬的典型组合。

汉代墓葬均为"甲"字形小砖室墓,坐南朝北,墓道方向大致相同,一般由墓道、前堂、后室三部分组成。另外有的墓葬由短甬道、双室和耳室组成。时代为西汉中、晚期至东汉晚期。

聭城寨墓地为战国和汉代两个时期相互重叠的家族墓地,排列有序。墓葬下有仰韶、西周时期的文化层,说明古代人类在仰韶文化和周朝时期曾在此活动。特别是出土的五层彩绘陶楼、陶仓楼保存完好,丰富了陶楼的研究资料。聭城寨墓地的发掘为研究豫西北焦作一带战国和汉代的埋葬制度和习俗提供了重要的实物资料。

陶仓楼（2006MCM1:1）　　　　Pottery storage building

汉　　　　　　　　　　　　　　Han

高 73.5、面阔 62、进深 17 厘米　Height 73.5cm, front width 62cm,

　　　　　　　　　　　　　　　depth from front to rear 17cm

The Kuichengzhai cemetery is located in northwestern Kuichengzhai, Jiulishan town, Macun district of Jiaozuo city. It covers an area of more than 42 ha. Henan Provincial Institute of Cultural Relics and archaeology excavated the cemetery from May to December of 2006. The excavated area is 3700 square meters. The excavation revealed 33 Warring States, Han, and Qing tombs, 32 pits, and 3 ditches, and collected a large number of artifacts from the Warring States, Han, and Yangshao periods.

All of the Warring States tombs are rectangular vertical shaft tombs. The body position varied and included face-up, face-down, and flexed bodies resting on a side. The composition of pottery includes a Ding tripod, a Dou, and a pot, the typical assemblage of grave goods for a small tomb of the middle Warring States period.

The Han tombs are all small brick-chambered tombs with plane looks resembling the Chinese word "Jia". All of them face south and have the same direction of their passages. These tombs are generally composed of a passage, an antechamber and a post-chamber. Some tombs consist of a short corridor, a double chamber, and an ear chamber. They are dated to the middle and late Western Han and late Eastern Han.

The Kuichengzhai cemetery is a family cemetery, in which burials from Warring States and Han periods superposed each other. Under the cemetery there are the deposits of Yangshao and Western Zhou periods. The well-preserved painted pottery building and storage building with five tiers enrich the research materials on pottery buildings. The excavation at Kuichengzhai provides important materials for investigating the burial system and custom in northwest Henan in the Warring States and Han periods.

彩绘五层陶楼（2006MK1 M19:1）
汉
高 126、面阔 83、进深 50.5 厘米；
院长 25.5、宽 55、高 24 厘米；
门架高 4.5、门高 19、宽 12.5 厘米

Painted pottery building with five tiers
Han
Height 126cm, front width 83cm, depth from front to rear 50.5cm
Yard length 25.5cm, width 55cm, height 24cm
Door frame height 4.5cm, door height 19cm, width 12.5cm

徐堡城址
Xubao City-site

　　徐堡龙山文化城址位于焦作市温县武德镇徐堡村东，沁河南岸。2006年8月，洛阳市文物工作队、焦作市文物工作队对其进行了考古发掘，发掘面积2000平方米。发现了龙山时代的城墙、壕沟、大型台基等遗迹现象，出土器物100余件。遗址文化层堆积厚约4米，为龙山、西周、春秋、战国、汉、宋、明、清8个时期连续叠压。

　　龙山城址遗存主要有城墙、壕沟、台基、灰坑、墓葬、陶窑等。城址平面略呈圆角长方形，现存面积约20万平方米。城墙为堆筑夯打而成，西、南、东三面城墙保存较好，墙体两侧有护坡3~4层。西城墙长360、南墙长500、东墙长约200米，北墙被沁河冲毁。在西墙和东墙的中部各有一缺口，宽约10米左右，应为城门所在。在城址中部发现一处堆筑台基，东西长90、南北宽70米，面积6000余平方米，可能为城址的重要建筑部位。清理龙山时期灰坑11座，墓葬1座，陶窑1座。灰坑为圆形和椭圆形，H88为圆形桶状，坑底打在城墙护坡上，属典型龙山晚期遗迹。墓葬出土遗物以陶器为主，主要有深腹罐、圈足盘、刻槽盆、钵、器盖等。

　　西周文化遗存遍布整个发掘区，共发掘灰坑33座，居址柱洞5处，灶坑1座，祭祀坑8座。春秋、战国文化遗存有灰坑3座，墓葬3座，灶坑1座，排水沟1条。汉代遗存有空心砖和小砖残墓3座，灰坑1座，灰沟1条。宋代遗存有砖室墓2座，竖穴土洞墓3座，灰坑2座。明、清时期遗存有窖藏坑30座，墓葬25座，水井5口。

　　徐堡龙山城址是目前黄河流域所发现的龙山文化城址中保存较好、规模较大的一座城址，为豫西北地区首次发现，为研究史前城址聚落形态、文明起源、国家的形成、筑城技术等诸多问题提供了重要的实物资料。

陶鬲（M67:1）　　　　Pottery Li
周　　　　　　　　　Zhou
高 9.5、口径 13 厘米　Height 9.5cm, rim diameter 13cm

陶盘（H280:4）
新石器时代（龙山文化）
高 12.3、口径 37、圈足径 26 厘米

Pottery dish
Neolithic Age (Longshan culture)
Height 12.3cm, rim diameter 37cm, diameter of circular base 26cm

The Longshan cultural city site of Xubao is located in eastern Xubao village, Wude town in Wenxian, Jiaozuo city, southern bank of the Qin River. The current preserved area is about 20 ha. Luoyang Municipal Team of Archaeology, and Jiaozuo Municipal Team of Archaeology excavated the site in August 2006, and uncovered 2000 square meters. The city wall, a ditch, and a large platform foundation were unearthed, and more than 100 artifacts were collected. The depth of cultural deposits is about 4 meters and includes relics from Longshan, Western Zhou, Eastern Zhou, Han, Song, Ming and Qing periods. The features mainly include city walls, ditches, platform foundations, ash pits, tombs, and pottery kilns. The plan of the site is generally rectangular with round corner. The city walls were rammed and western, southern and eastern walls were well preserved. There are protective slopes, 3-4 meters thick, on both sides of the walls. The length of western wall is 360m, while the southern wall is 500m long, and the eastern wall is 200m long. The northern wall was damaged by the Qin River. Two gaps were found respectively in western and eastern walls. Each gap is about 10 meters wide. These gaps likely demarcate the lo-

鹿角（H118 ⑥:1）
新石器时代（龙山文化）
残长 36 厘米

Deer antler
Neolithic Age (Longshan culture)
Incomplete length 36cm

cation of city gates. One platform foundation was found in the center of the city. It is 90m in west-east direction, 70m in north-south direction, and more than 6000 square meters in area. This foundation likely marks the location of a principal building of the city. Eleven pits, one burial, and one pottery kiln dating to the Longshan culture were recovered. The offerings from the burial mostly included jars, dishes, basins, bowls and lids. The Western Zhou remains were distributed in the whole excavated area, and 33 pits, 5 post holes, one stove pit and 8 sacrificial pits were uncovered. The Spring and Autumn and Warring States features include 3 pits, 3 burials, one stove pit and one barrel-drain. There are 3 tombs, one pit, and one ash ditch dating to Han Dynasty, 5 tombs and 2 pits to the Song Dynasty, and 30 cache pits, 25 burials and 5 wells to the Ming and Qing Dynasty.

The Xubao city site is a large and well-preserved Longshan city revealed so far in the Yellow River valley. It is the first Longshan city found in northwest Henan, and provides important materials for investigating the patterns of city sites, the origins of civilization, the formation of early states, and the technology for building cities in the prehistory.

聂村墓地

Niecun cemetery

　　聂村墓地位于焦作市博爱县阳庙镇聂村周围，县级文物保护单位。2006年7~10月，洛阳市文物工作队、焦作市文物工作队对聂村墓群进行了考古勘探和发掘，发掘面积2300平方米，清理唐、宋、明、清墓葬22座，灰坑10个，古道路2条，出土一批唐三彩、瓷器、铜器、纪年墓志等70多件珍贵文物，取得了重要考古收获。

　　唐代墓葬13座，为本次发掘的重要发现。墓葬均为砖室墓，分正方形单室墓、长方形单室墓、双室墓和砖棺墓四种。各墓葬所出器物种类、数量不同，主要有三彩钵、三彩罐、三彩碗、铜洗、铜镜、银手镯、铜戒指、青釉瓷瓶、青釉瓷碗、陶俑、陶骆驼、陶马、陶罐、开元通宝、乾隆通宝铜钱等。其中4件三彩钵为巩县

黄冶窑生产的标准三彩器（咸亨二年至天宝元年盛唐时期，即671~742年），其制作工艺精良，是唐三彩中的精品之作。出土的四神十二生肖镜、花鸟菱花镜、仙骑镜，图案布局和谐、制作精良，反映了盛唐时期高超的制镜工艺。绿釉三彩罐、青釉洒金三彩碗及蚌壳等珍贵文物，具有极高的文物价值。M5出土有纪年墓志，记载墓主为咸亨二年（671年）唐骑尉向君及夫人。

　　焦作地区隋唐时期为河内郡及怀州，属黄河以北通往东都洛阳的交通要道，属繁华之地。纪年唐墓的发掘及珍贵文物的出土，为研究焦作地区唐墓的形制、葬俗以及盛唐时期焦作地区的经济文化、社会发展提供了实物依据。

三彩钵（M5:1）
唐
高 12.8、口径 14.3 厘米

Tricolor bowl
Tang
Height 12.8cm, rim diameter 14.3cm

The Niecun cemetery is located near Niecun, Yangmiao town in Boai county, Jiaozuo city. Luoyang Municipal Team of Archaeology, and Jiaozuo Municipal Team of Archaeology excavated the cemetery from July to October of 2006. The excavation area is 2300 square meters. Twenty-two burials, 10 ash pits and 2 roads dating to Tang, Song, Ming and Qing periods were revealed, and over 70 artifacts including Tang tricolor pottery, porcelain, bronze vessels, annals epitaphs were collected.

Thirteen Tang tombs are all brick-chambered tombs, including square single-chambered, rectangular single-chambered, double-chambered and brick-coffin categories. Different tombs unearthed different kinds and numbers of grave goods, mostly including tricolor Bo, a bowl and a jar, a bronze Xi, a mirror and a finger ring, a silver bracelet, a celadon porcelain vase and a bowl, a pottery figurine, a camel, a horse, and a jar, as well as Kaiyuan Tongbao and Qianlong

Tongbao coins. Of these, four tricolor Bo, the standard vessels made by Huangye kiln in Gongxian in the flourishing Tang Dynasty (AD 671-742) are the most exquisite artifacts. The bronze mirror with four deities and twelve animals representing the twelve Earthly Branches, diamond-shaped mirror with flower and bird design, and a mirror with celestial cavalry reflect the advanced technique of mirror-making in the flourishing Tang Dynasty. Tricolor jar with green glaze, tricolor bowl with green glaze and splashed gold and shell are precious artifacts.

Jiaozuo region belonged to Henei shire and Huai state during the Sui and Tang Dynasties, and was the main place toward Luoyang, the eastern Capital, from the north of the Yellow River. The finding of Tang tombs with annals epitaph and precious artifacts provides important information for investigating the form, burial custom of Tang tombs, as well as the economy, culture, and society in Jiaozuo region during the flourishing Tang Dynasty.

陶俑组合（M5）　　　　Pottery figurines
唐　　　　　　　　　　Tang
高 15.5~28 厘米　　　　Heights 15.5-28cm

陶俑（M5:9）
唐
高 28 厘米

Pottery figurine
Tang
Height 28cm

三彩钵（M6:3）
唐
高 16、口径 15 厘米

Tricolor bowl
Tang
Height 16cm, rim diameter 15cm

山后墓地

Shanhou cemetery

　　山后墓地位于焦作市马村区九里山乡山后村的西南部。2006年7~9月,洛阳市文物工作队对墓地进行了发掘,发掘面积约800平方米,共清理汉代墓葬7座,出土了一批汉代陶器和铜器。

　　汉墓均为带墓道的砖室墓,墓室底部铺砖,墓壁单砖错缝平铺,可分为前后双室墓和单室墓两种。双室墓顶部破坏严重。单室墓有单室带耳室墓和无耳室墓,室顶有穹窿顶和券顶两种。单室墓的墓室前有一道封门墙,一般用砖筑,个别用大石块代替。墓葬均为坐南朝北,墓道有长斜坡式和竖井式两种。其中M4形制比较特别,其墓道和墓室的宽度基本相同,券顶保存完好,其券顶的砖缝间插有陶片,以保证券顶的坚固。遗物主要有陶鼎、罐、壶、瓮、耳杯、魁、灶、猪圈等,个别墓中还出土了五铢钱以及铜节约等小型青铜构件。这批汉墓时代为西汉晚期到东汉晚期。

陶俑（M7:1）　　　　Pottery figurine
汉　　　　　　　　　Han
高11.6、宽6.7厘米　　Height 11.6cm, width 6.7cm

陶猪圈（M4:6）　　　　　　Pottery sty
汉　　　　　　　　　　　　Han
高 14.5、直径 26.3 厘米　　Height 14.5cm, diameter 26.3cm

陶狗（M7:2）　　　　　　Pottery dog
汉　　　　　　　　　　　Han
高 6.5、长 19.1、　　　　Height 6.5cm, length 19.1cm,
宽 7.3 厘米　　　　　　　width 7.3cm

The Shanhou cemetery is located in the southwest Shanhou village, Jiulishan town, Macun district of Jiaozuo city. Luoyang Municipal Team of Archaeology excavated the cemetery from July to September of 2006. The excavation area is about 800 square meters. Seven tombs were revealed and unearthed a large number of pottery and bronze vessels.

The Han tombs are all brick-chambered tombs with tomb passage. The bottom of chamber was paved with bricks. The wall was flatly paved by the method of single-brick and stagger-gap. The tombs can be classified into two categories, double-chambered and single-chambered tombs. The roofs of double-chambered tombs were severely damaged. The single-chambered tombs include single-chambered tombs with and without side chamber. There is a wall to close down tomb gate in the front of single-chambered tombs. Most of them were built with bricks and very few were built with big stones. All the tombs face north with long and slope passage, or vertical passage. The offering objects mainly include a pottery Ding tripod, a jar, a pot, an urn, a cup, a Kui, a stove and a sty. Some tombs unearthed Wuzhu coins and a bronze Jieyue. These tombs date to the period from the late Western Han to late Eastern Han.

苏王墓地

Suwang cemetery

苏王墓地位于焦作市温县北冷乡北冷村,南距县城5公里,地势平坦开阔。2006年6~11月,洛阳市文物工作队会同焦作市文物勘探队对墓地进行了勘探和发掘。发掘面积3800平方米,清理墓葬96座。其中宋代墓葬38座,明代墓葬58座,包括砖券墓11座,瓦券墓1座,砖瓦混券墓1座,竖穴土坑及洞室墓83座,明代正统四年(1439年)纪年墓葬1座。随葬品少见,有砖质买地券、砖雕、琉璃簪、铜钱、铁犁铧等106件。

宋代墓葬可分为砖室墓和土坑竖穴墓两种。砖室墓均为单室穹窿顶,除一座墓葬朝向东南外,皆坐北朝南,分竖穴、阶梯墓道两种。墓室分为长方形、方形、六角形,砌筑方法基本相同,墓壁均为单砖错缝平砌。穹窿顶为叠涩砌法,分圆形顶和覆斗形顶两种。土坑竖穴墓皆为长方形,南北方向。葬具均为单棺,已腐朽。葬式均为

夫妻二次迁葬墓,墓内骨架多少不等,一般为二人合葬,也有一夫二妻、三妻合葬。随葬品极少,有砖雕、铜钱、铁犁铧、陶罐。二次葬是该墓地宋墓的一大特点。

明代墓葬可分砖券单室墓、竖穴墓道洞室墓和土坑竖穴墓三种,皆坐北朝南。从墓葬的排列位置和墓向看应为家族墓地。砖室墓均为长方形券顶。竖穴墓道洞室墓,墓道的长和宽均大于墓室,在墓道内墓门的两侧各有一方形生土台,形似门墩。土坑竖穴墓皆为长方形,南北方向。葬具均为单棺,已腐朽,葬式为仰身直肢,头向北。随葬品极少,有琉璃簪、铜钱,个别墓葬有买地券,其中一座纪年墓为明代正统四年。

通过勘探发掘,基本搞清了苏王墓地的基本情况,虽然出土物不丰富,但是不同的墓葬形制、葬俗为研究当地宋、明时期家族墓地的埋葬习俗和埋葬制度提供了丰富的实物资料。

砖雕机壶（M2:4）　宋　长28.8、宽14.1、厚4.1厘米
Brick-carved pot　Song　Length 28.8cm, width 14.1cm, depth 4.1cm

砖雕熨斗（M2:2）
宋
长 28.9、宽 14.1、厚 4.4 厘米

Brick-carved flatiron
Song
Length 28.9cm, width 14.1cm, depth 4.4cm

The Suwang cemetery is located in northern Beileng village, Beileng town in Wenxian, Jiaozuo city. Luoyang Municipal Team of Archaeology and Jiaozuo Municipal Team of Archaeology excavated the cemetery from June to November of 2006. The excavation revealed 96 tombs in 3800 square meters. Of these tombs, 38 date to Song, and 58 to Ming. Most of them are shaft and cavity-chambered tombs. The number of collected artifacts is 106, including brick certificates of buying terra, carved bricks, colored glaze hairpins, bronze coins, and iron ploughs.

The Song tombs can be classified into brick-chambered and shaft tombs. All of the brick-chambered tombs are single arched-roof. Most of the tombs face south. Tomb chambers in shape witness rectangular, square, and hexagon. Tomb walls were all built by laying bricks with stagger gap. The roofs have round and inverted-cup-shaped categories. Shaft tombs are all rectangular in north-south direction. All of the burial furniture are single coffin and were moldered. The tombs are all secondary burials of couple. Human skeletons in each tomb are not equal. Most of the tombs have two skeletons, some have one male and two or three females. The number of offering objects is very few. They are carved bricks, coins, iron ploughs

砖雕茶杯（M2:5）
宋
长 14.6、宽 14.3、厚 4.4 厘米

Brick-carved cup
Song
Length 14.6cm, width 14.3cm,
depth 4.4cm

and pottery jars.

The Ming tombs can be divided into three categories, brick-arched single tomb, cavity-chambered tomb with vertical passage, and shaft tomb. All of the tombs face south. According to arrangement position and direction of tombs, these tombs should belong to a family cemetery. All the brick-chambered tombs are rectangular arched-roof tombs. The length and width of passage for cavity-chambered tombs are bigger than that of chamber. There is a square earth platform in each side of tomb gate like a gate frusta. Shaft tombs are all rectangular in north-south direction. All of the burial furniture are single coffin and were moldered. The burial manner is extended burial with head northward. Offering objects are very few, including colored glaze hairpins, bronze coins and brick certificates of buying terra. One annals tomb indicates the Fouth Year of Zhengtong in the Ming Dynasty.

It is generally clear about the plan of the Suwang cemetery through drilling and excavation. The unearthed artifacts are not rich, but different burial forms and customs provide rich materials for a study of burial custom and system of family cemetery in the region in the Song and Ming Dynasties.

西金城遗址
Xijincheng site

西金城遗址位于博爱县金城乡西金城村的中东部。2006~2007年，山东大学考古队对西金城遗址进行了大规模发掘，发掘面积5200平方米。发现龙山文化城址1座，取得了重要考古成果。

西金城龙山文化城址大部分压在村舍之下，城墙埋于地下1.5米，残高2~3米。城址的平面形状大致呈圆角长方形，面积达30.8万平方米，北墙长560、西墙长520、南墙长400、东墙长440米，

陶罐（H126:5）　新石器时代（龙山文化）　高35.5、口径12.4、底径10.5厘米
Pottery jar　Neolithic Age (Longshan culture)　Height 35.5cm, rim diameter 12.4cm, base diameter 10.5cm

石刀 （T0804 ⑤ C:6）
新石器时代（龙山文化）
残长 7.2、宽 3.9、厚 0.7 厘米

Stone knife
Neolithic Age (Longshan culture)
Incomplete length 7.2cm, width 3.9cm,
depth 0.7cm

北、西墙宽 20 米左右，东墙宽 10 米左右，南墙宽度介于二者之间。在西、南墙中部可能有城门，北、东、南墙外侧发现有小河或排水沟环绕形成的防御壕沟。城址废弃于河南龙山文化晚期，建筑年代应在龙山文化中期前后，距今 4000 多年前。

通过系统钻探和大规模发掘可知，在西、东墙外分别发现大面积的沼泽堆积和缓土岗，土岗高处有小片龙山时期的居住堆积，在居住堆积的灰坑中浮选出粟、黍、水稻、小麦和大豆等粮食作物的炭化遗存，推测城外的沼泽和缓土岗应是种植这些粮食作物的生产经济区，缓土岗的高处则是从事季节性生产的临时住地。另外，在城内东南角还发现较大面积的高土岗，岗上的龙山文化堆积深厚，居住遗迹密集，很可能是

贵族居住区，城内其他部分文化堆积略薄，应是平民居住区。

西金城龙山文化城址有较丰富的文化遗存，包括大量生产劳作工具的残断石器和部分生活器具陶器，以及丰富的采捞田螺壳和少量猪、狗、鹿等哺乳动物遗骸。陶器种类主要为罐、豆、壶、鬶、斝、甗、盆、双腹盆、刻槽盆、单耳杯和鼎等，石器种类主要有刀、镰、铲等，整体文化面貌属于河南龙山文化（王湾三期文化）的中晚期。

本次对该城址的发掘，使我们对周围古地貌和经济生产区有了一个系统的认识，也是河南省对其他龙山城址以往考古工作的新突破，尤其小麦遗存在河南境内龙山文化遗址中的首次发现，对研究小麦在我国的出现和传播路线以及中原地区文明起源阶段的人地关系演变，都具有重要学术价值。

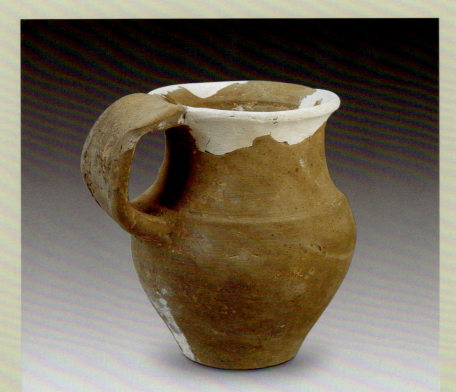

陶单耳杯（M98:2）
新石器时代（龙山文化）
高12、口径8、底径5.3厘米

Pottery cup with single handle
Neolithic Age (Longshan culture)
Height 12cm, rim diameter 8cm, base diameter 5.3cm

The Xijincheng site is located in the mid-east part of Xijincheng village, Jincheng town in Boai county. The Archaeological Team of Shandong University excavated the site in 2006 and 2007. The excavation area is 5200 square meters. The excavation revealed one city site of the Longshan culture.

The city site was mostly covered by the modern village. The city wall is underground 1.5m, and remains 2-3m in height. The plane of city site is generally rectangular with round corner. It is 30.8 ha in area and the length for north wall is 560m, 520m for west wall, 400 for south wall, and 440m for east wall. The width of north and west is around 20m, and that of east wall is 10m. The width of south wall falls into 10-20m. There may have been city gates in the middle of west and south walls. A small river or barrel-drain was found outside the north, east and south walls. The city site was abandoned in the late Longshan period. The building age should be around 4000 years ago, dating to the middle Longshan period.

By systematical drilling and excavation, a large area of swamp and earth hillock was found outside the west and east walls. There are some habitation deposits on the top of the hillock. Millet, rice, wheat, and soybean remains were collected by flotation from the ash pits in the habitation area, suggesting that the swamp and earth hillock should be the economic area for production crops, and the top of the hillock many have been the temporary habitation area for seasonal production. Moreover, a large area of hillock was revealed in the southeastern corner of the city. The Longshan cultural deposits are thick and habitation features are dense, indicating that there may have been the noble habitation area. The thin deposits in the rest of the city may have been the civil habitation area.

The city site unearthed a large number of artifacts, including stone tools and pottery vessels, as well as faunal remains such as pigs, dogs and deer. Pottery vessels are mainly jars, Dou, pots, basins, double-belly basins, groove-carved basins, cups with single handle, and Ding tripods. Stone tools include knives, sickles and shovels. The cultural characteristic belongs to the middle and late Henan Longshan culture (Wangwan III culture).

The excavation at the city site sheds light on our understanding of palaeo-physiognomy and economic production area. It is a new breakthrough in the study of Longshan

石斧（采集:5）
新石器时代（龙山文化）
残长 11.8、宽 4.5、厚 4.5 厘米

Stone axe
Neolithic Age (Longshan culture)
Incomplete length 11.8cm, width 4.5cm, depth 4.5cm

city site in Henan. In particular, the first finding of wheat in Henan Longshan site is of important academic value in investigating the emergence and diffusive route of wheat in China, as well as the relationship between humans and environment during the period of emergent civilization in the Central Plain.

石铲（H139:1）
新石器时代（龙山文化）
残长 10.5、宽 9.3、厚 1.3 厘米

Stone shovel
Neolithic Age (Longshan culture)
Incomplete length 10.5cm, width 9.3cm,
depth 1.3cm

石铲（T0704 ⑤ B:3）
新石器时代（龙山文化）
残长 11.1、宽 9、厚 1.1 厘米

Stone shovel
Neolithic Age (Longshan culture)
Incomplete length 11.1cm, width 9cm,
depth 1.1cm

石镰（T0602 ⑤ B:4）
新石器时代（龙山文化）
长 21、宽 5.5、厚 0.8 厘米

Stone sickle
Neolithic Age (Longshan culture)
Length 21cm, width 5.5cm, depth 0.8cm

郑州

娘娘寨遗址

Niangniangzhai site

娘娘寨遗址位于荥阳市豫龙镇寨杨村西北约200米处,遗址北面索河环绕而过,遗址中心现存有一个高出周围约3米的台地,台地周边保留有夯土城墙。2004年底至2005年初,郑州市文物考古研究院对其进行了考古调查及钻探,确认娘娘寨遗址是一个有重大考古价值的古城址,具有十分重要的学术意义。遗址范围为南北长约1000、东西宽约500米,总面积逾50万平方米,南水北调干渠占压10万平方米。同时,经钻探发现该城址外有一宽近50米的护城河,该护城河最深处达8米,加上城址土台高度可达12米,绕城址一周。

娘娘寨遗址考古发掘至2007年底,共发掘面积约13000平方米,清理各类遗迹1600多个,遗迹主要有城墙、夯土基址、墓葬、灰坑、陶窑、水井、灰沟、土灶等。其中城墙为西周时期;夯土基址目前揭露7处,分东周和西周两个时期;墓葬、陶窑多为西周时期;灰坑发现有1640多个,多为东周时期,西周时期约占五分之一。钻探发现在城址内分布有南北向、东西向两条道路,道路宽2~3米。城址中部、东南部分布有大规模的夯土基址,在城址西北部分布有较多的陶窑,为城址的作坊区。目前钻探仍在进行中。出土遗物多为陶器,有石器、骨器、蚌器以及小型铜器、玉器等。陶器种类多为罐、盆、豆、鬲、瓮、簋等。

玉璜(M13:1)
西周
长9.7、宽3.9、厚0.45厘米

Jade Huang
Western Zhou
Length 9.7cm, width 3.9cm, depth 0.45cm

娘娘寨遗址从目前发掘情况来看，其文化遗存大的分期可分为五期，即河南龙山文化晚期、二里头文化、西周、春秋、战国。其中河南龙山文化晚期遗存太少，不可再细分；二里头文化遗存发现较少，为二里头文化晚期。娘娘寨遗址西周文化地层被春秋战国时期的遗存破坏殆尽，基本不见，多以坑状和墓葬等单位遗迹为主，从所出遗物特征来看，传统的西周文化早、中、晚三期均有，器物组合为鬲、罐、豆、盆、瓮等；其中西周早期遗存较少，遗物特征为早期偏晚；西周中晚期遗存相对较多。不过春秋战国时期的单位遗迹中大多发现有西周时期遗物，说明春秋战国时期人们在此活动频繁，将西周时期文化遗存扰乱，此次发掘发现有较多的铜箭镞，说明当时此地经常发生战争。娘娘寨遗址发掘出土了大量的春秋战国时期陶器，为该时期文化分期提供了大量实物，从器物特征来看，可细分为春秋早、中、晚和战国早、中、晚几个时期，具体尚有待于进一步整理确认。

娘娘寨遗址实为一个古城址，其文化内涵主要为西周和东周时期。据《左传》隐公元年（公元前722年）杜注云："虢叔，东虢君也……虢国，今荥阳县。'"《水经注·济水》云："索水又东，迳虢亭南，应劭曰：'荥阳，故国也，今

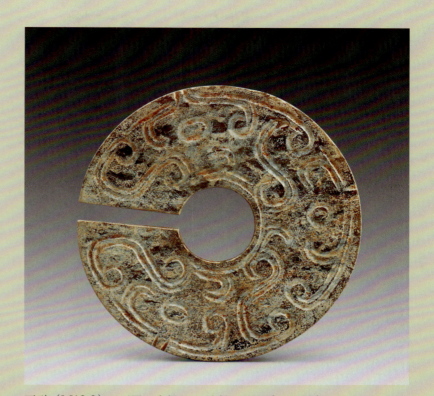

玉玦（M13:2）　西周　直径3.8、孔径1.02、厚0.25厘米
Jade Jue　Western Zhou　Diameter 3.8cm, orifice diameter 10.2cm, depth 0.25cm

虢亭是矣。'"可见，有众多文献记载西周初文王弟虢仲所封东虢国在荥阳境内。此外，《国语·郑语》载："其济洛、河、颍之间乎，是其子男之国，虢、郐为大，虢叔恃势，郐仲恃险。"而娘娘寨遗址北临索河，目前发现有西周时期的城墙，一宽近50、深达12米的护城河，发现有西周早、中、晚三个时期的遗存。尤其是发现有与都邑遗址相符的高规格遗存城墙和夯土基址。其地理位置、文化内涵、时代上均与东虢国相符，极有可能就是东虢国故址。如果推测无误，娘娘寨城址应是在郑州地区发现的第一座西周封国城址，具有十分重要的学术价值。

陶豆（M9:3）　西周　高 12.6、口径 15.5、
底径 10.3 厘米

Pottery Dou
Western Zhou
Height 12.6cm, rim diameter 155.5cm,
base diameter 10.3cm

陶鬲（M9:2）
西周
高 14、口径 19.2 厘米

Pottery Li
Western Zhou
Height 14cm, rim diameter 19.2cm

The Niangniangzhai site is located in northwestern Zhaiyang village, Yulong town in Xingyang, Zhengzhou. It is more than 50 ha. in area, 1000m long in north-south direction and 500m wide in west-east direction. The drilling work indicates that the site is a city site with a fifty-meters wide moat around the site. Zhengzhou Municipal Institute of Cultural Relics and Archaeology excavated the site in 2007. It is 1.3 ha. in excavation area. The excavation revealed more than 1600 various features, mainly including city walls, rammed foundations, burials, pits, pottery kilns, wells, earth stoves and so on. The city walls date to the Western Zhou, seven rammed foundations

to the Western and Eastern Zhou periods, most of the burials and pottery kilns to the Western Zhou, and most of the pits to the Western Zhou. The drilling work suggests that there are two roads with 2-3m width in the city. A large-scale of rammed foundation was found in the center and southeast part of the city. Many kilns were distributed in the northwest part of the city. It is the workshop area of the city. Unearthed artifacts include pottery, stone, bone, and shell artifacts, as well as small bronze and jade artifacts. The pottery vessels witness jars, basins, Dou, Li, urns, and Gui.

Based on the current excavation, the site can be divided into five periods: late Longshan culture,

Erlitou culture, Western Zhou, Spring and Autumn, and Warring States. The remains of Longshan and Erlitou cultures are very few, and the Western Zhou layers were severely disturbed by the activities of the Spring and Autumn and Warring States periods. The unearthed artifacts indicate that the Western Zhou culture can be divided into early, middle and late periods. The pottery vessels include Li, Jars, Dou, basins, and urns. The site unearthed a large number of pottery vessels dating to the Spring and Autumn and Warring States periods. The pottery vessels provide materials for cultural periodization.

The Niangniangzhai site is a Western Zhou and Eastern Zhou city site. Its location, cultural characteristic, and age are consistent with the Eastern Guo state, suggesting that this site is very likely to be the city of the Eastern Guo state. If the speculation is not wrong, the Niangniangzhai site should be the first Western Zhou city in Zhengzhou region, and is of important value for academic research.

陶盆（H350:1）
西周
高 14.5、口径 22.2、底径 13.1 厘米

Pottery basin
Western Zhou
Height 14.5cm, rim diameter 22.2cm, base diameter 13.1cm

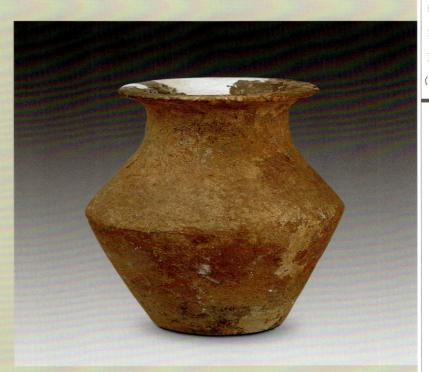

陶壶（M9:1）
西周
高 13.7、口径 11.1、底径 7.4 厘米

Pottery pot
Western Zhou
Height 13.7cm, rim diameter 11.1cm, base diameter 7.4cm

薛村遗址
Xuecun site

薛村遗址位于荥阳市王村乡薛村村北，遗址现存面积为50万平方米。遗址地处邙山南麓，北距黄河约0.8公里。2005~2006年河南省文物考古研究所继续对该遗址进行了大规模考古发掘，发掘面积20000平方米。发现夏商时期小型聚落和大量汉唐墓葬，出土了一大批精美的文物。遗址在夏代晚期至早商时期为一聚落点，至汉代沦为墓地，发现汉至清各时期墓葬450座，其中以汉墓和唐墓发现最多。

汉墓可分为大、中、小型三类。大型汉墓有长斜坡墓道，中小型汉墓多为竖穴墓道洞室墓。出土遗物以陶器为最多，其中以彩绘陶器和釉陶比较精美，诸如彩绘陶楼、彩绘灯熏、釉陶灯熏、绿釉或酱釉的铺首衔环陶壶、彩绘乐舞俑等。

陶深腹罐（H10:2）
夏代晚期（二里头文化晚期）
高31、口径23.8厘米

Pottery deep-belly jar
Late Xia Dynasty (late Erlitou culture)
Height 31cm, rim diameter 23.8cm

兽面纹器座（H132:001）
夏末商初
残长16.8、残宽22、厚1厘米

Pottery pedestal with animal mask motif
Late Xia and early Shang
Incomplete length 16.8cm, incomplete width 22cm,
depth 1cm

　　唐代墓葬从初唐到晚唐都有发现，年代序列基本完整。出土器物一般为瓷器、红陶或白陶的彩绘俑以及具有浓郁生活气息的模型明器，另有少量的漆木器和铜镜。代表性的遗物有白釉塔式罐、彩绘红陶或白陶的天王、镇墓兽、骑马俑、文吏俑、武士俑、仕女俑、胡俑、牛及牛车、鸡、狗等。其中出土的一匹白釉瓷马，制作精美异常。另外出土有石质或砖质的墓志8合，以线刻海石榴花、围绕四神十二生肖的石墓志最有代表性。

　　隋代、北宋、金代、元代以及明清墓葬出土有黄釉瓶、绿釉枕、白釉罐、花釉碗、青花瓷碗、环形小玉口琀。

　　薛村遗址的汉代和唐代墓葬数量多，分布密集，具有家族墓地的特点，并且已经辨认出有唐代李氏家族墓。该遗址墓地从西汉晚期开始使用，历东汉、隋、唐、北宋、金、元、明、清，纵向时间跨度大，时代序列较为完整，为研究汉、唐时期家族墓地及其丧葬制度以及中国传统丧葬文化演变传承和邙山墓葬区的形成、发展，提供了重要的实物资料。

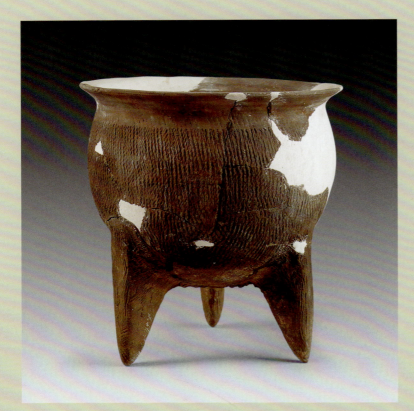

夹砂灰陶鼎（T11 ②:1）
商代早期
高 34、口径 31.4 厘米

Grey pottery Ding tripod with mixed sand
Early Shang
Height 34cm, rim diameter 31.4cm

The Xuecun site, 50 ha. in area, is located in northern Xuecun, Wangcun town in Xingyang city, the southern foot of Mang Mountain, close to the Yellow River. Henan Provincial Institute of Cultural Relics and Archaeology excavated the site in 2005 and 2006. The excavation area is 2 ha. The excavation revealed a small settlement dating to Xia and Shang periods and a large number of Han and Tang tombs, and unearthed a large quantity of exquisite artifacts. A total of 450 tombs ranging from Han to Qing periods were excavated. Of these, Han and Tang tombs dominate the assemblage.

The Han tombs can be divided into large, medium and small categories. The large tomb has a long and slop passage, and most of the medium and small tombs are cavity-chambered tombs. Most of the offering objects are pottery vessels, of which painted pottery and glazed pottery vessels are exquisite, such as painted pottery building, painted pottery incense lamp, glazed pottery incense lamp, green glaze or brown glaze pottery pot with beast head holding a loose ring, painted figurine of musician and dancer.

The Tang tombs range from the early to late Tang, and chronology is generally complete. The unearthed objects mainly include porcelain, red or white pottery figurines, funerary objects, lacquer vessels and bronze mirrors. The typical artifacts are a white glazed porcelain jar in tower shape, a painted red or white pottery celestial king, an animality patron in tomb, a figurine with a rider on a horse, a figurine of civil official, a figurine of warrior, a figurine of waitress, a figurine of non-Han nationality, cattle and oxcarts, a chicken, a dog and so on. The Sui, Northern Song, Jin Yuan and Ming-Qing tombs unearthed a yellow glazed porcelain vase, a green glazed porcelain pillow, a white glazed jar, a multi-color glaze bowl, and a blue-and-white porcelain bowl.

The number and density of the Han and Tang tombs at the Xuecun site indicate that the cemetery may have been a family cemetery. The cemetery was occupied from the late Western Han, through the Eastern Han, Sui, Tang, Northern Song, Jin, Yuan, Ming, and Qing. The chronology is complete and covers a long period of time. The excavation provides important materials for investigating Han and Tang family cemeteries and their burial systems, as well as the change and succession of burial cultures in ancient China and the formation and development of Mangshan burial area.

陶鬲 （M30:2）

商代早期

高 21、口径 17.5 厘米

Pottery Li

Early Shang

Height 21cm, rim diameter 17.5cm

石圭首铲（H311:1）
商代早期
长 33、宽 8.8 厘米

Stone shovel with Gui-shaped head
Early Shang
Length 33cm, width 8.8cm

彩绘陶鼎（M28:48）

汉

通高 25.2、口径 14、底径 11.8 厘米

Painted pottery Ding tripod

Han

Height 25.2cm, rim diameter 14cm, base diameter 11.8cm

陶尊（M45:5）
汉
高 15.5、口径 15.4、
底径 16.5 厘米

Pottery Zun
Han
Height 15.5cm, rim diameter 15.4cm,
base diameter 16.5cm

灰陶带猪圈厕（M66:8）
汉
高 16、长 24、宽 22 厘米

Gray pottery lavatory with sty
Han
Height 16cm, length 24cm, width 22cm

灰陶彩绘卧羊尊（M84:9）
汉
高 19.8、长 43.5、宽 16 厘米

Gray painted pottery Zun in crouching sheep shape
Han
Height 19.8cm, length 43.5cm, width 16cm

彩绘男俳优俑（M11:24）

汉

高 16.6 厘米

Painted male figurine

Han

Height 16.6cm

彩绘女俳优俑（M11:37）
汉
高 16.4 厘米

Painted female figurine
Han
Height 16.4cm

绿釉铺首衔环陶壶（M34:12）

汉

高 38.5、口径 14、底径 15 厘米

Green glazed pottery pot with beast head
holding a loose ring

Han

Height 38.5cm, rim diameter 14cm, base diameter
15cm

绿釉双层陶熏灯（M13:1）
汉
高 37 厘米

Green glazed pottery incense lamp with
double tier
Han
Height 37cm

铜镜（M17:32）　　　Bronze mirror
汉　　　　　　　　　　Han
直径 13 厘米　　　　　Diameter 13cm

白瓷塔式罐（M61:1）
唐
高 41、口径 8.8、底径 14.6 厘米

White porcelain jar in tower shape
Tang
Height 41cm, rim diameter 8.8cm, base
diameter 14.6cm

花釉瓷双系罐（M64:4）
唐
高 14.8、口径 9.4、底径 8.5 厘米

Multi-colored glazed porcelain jar
with two loops at neck
Tang
Height 14.8cm, rim diameter 9.4cm, base
diameter 8.5cm

花釉瓷执壶（M36:9）
唐
高 21.5、口径 9、底径 10 厘米

Multi-colored glazed porcelain vase with handle at the side
Tang
Height 21.5cm, rim diameter 9cm, base diameter 10cm

黄釉绞胎木纹瓷枕（M121:2）
唐
高 8、长 14.8、宽 11 厘米

Yellow Glazed porcelain pillow with
twisted paste and wooden design
Tang
Height 8cm, length 14.8cm, width 11cm

三彩执壶（M68:9）
唐
高 9.1、口径 3.5、底径 4 厘米

Tricolor vase with handle at the side
Tang
Height 9.1cm, rim diameter 3.5cm, base diameter 4cm

彩绘红陶人面镇墓兽（M5:6）
唐
高 46、宽 20.3 厘米

Painted red pottery animality patron
in tomb with human face
Tang
Height 46cm, width 20.3cm

彩绘红陶兽面镇墓兽（M5:3）
唐
高 45.5、宽 20.5 厘米

Painted red pottery animality
patron in tomb with animal face
Tang
Height 45.5cm, width 20.5cm

陶镇墓兽（M3:7）
唐
高 48.5 厘米

Pottery animality
patron in tomb
Tang
Height 48.5cm

陶镇墓兽（M3:6）
唐
高 55.5 厘米

Pottery animality
patron in tomb
Tang
Height 55.5cm

彩绘红陶天王俑（M3:4）
唐
高 60、宽 20.5 厘米

Painted red pottery figurine of
celestial horse
Tang
Height 60cm, width 20.5cm

彩绘红陶天王俑（M3:5）
唐
高 59.5、宽 18 厘米

Painted red pottery figurine of
celestial horse
Tang
Height 59.5cm, width 18cm

彩绘白陶文史俑（M68:6）
唐
高 48.6、宽 11.6 厘米

Painted white pottery figurine of
civil official
Tang
Height 48.6cm, width 11.6cm

彩绘白陶武士俑
（M68:19）
唐
高 48.6、宽 13.8 厘米

Painted white pottery figurine
of warrior
Tang
Height 48.6cm, width 13.8cm

陶武士俑（M141:40）
唐
高 67.5 厘米

Pottery figurine of warrior
Tang
Height 67.5cm

彩绘白陶侍女俑（M68:14）
唐
高 19.6、宽 5 厘米

Painted white pottery figurine of
female servant
Tang
Height 19.6cm, width 5cm

彩绘白陶仕女俑（M68:1）
唐
高 24.8、宽 8 厘米

Painted white pottery figurine of
female servant
Tang
Height 24.8cm, width 8cm

彩绘贴花白陶马（M68:7）
唐
高 40、长 37.5、宽 14.5 厘米

Painted white pottery horse with applied floral design
Tang
Height 40cm, length 37.5cm, width 14.5cm

白釉瓷马（M68:8）
唐
高 31.5、长 37.8 厘米

White glazed porcelain horse
Tang
Height 31.5cm, length 37.8cm

彩绘白陶马（M4:24）
唐
高 45.5、长 45、宽 18 厘米

Painted white pottery horse
Tang
Height 45.5cm, length 45cm, width 18cm

彩绘白陶枣红马（M4:25）

唐

高 46、长 45.8、宽 17.5 厘米

Painted white pottery horse in jujube red

Tang

Height 46cm, length 45.8cm, width 17.5cm

陶俑（M4:4）
唐
高 33.5 厘米

Pottery figurine
Tang
Height 33.5cm

彩绘白陶牵马俑（M4:11）
唐
高 33.6、宽 11.3 厘米

Painted white pottery figurine of
pulling horse
Tang
Height 33.6cm, width 11.3cm

陶骑马俑（M4:29）
唐
通高 41、马身长 32 厘米

Pottery figurine of riding horse
Tang
Height 41cm, length 32cm

彩绘白陶女骑马俑（M4:30）
唐
高40、残长30.5、宽14厘米

Painted white pottery female figurine
of riding horse
Tang
Height 40cm, incomplete length 30.5cm,
width 14cm

彩绘白陶男子骑马俑
（M4:28）
唐
高 39、残长 32.4、宽 14 厘米

**Painted white pottery male figurine
of riding horse**
Tang
Height 39cm, incomplete 32.4cm,
width 14cm

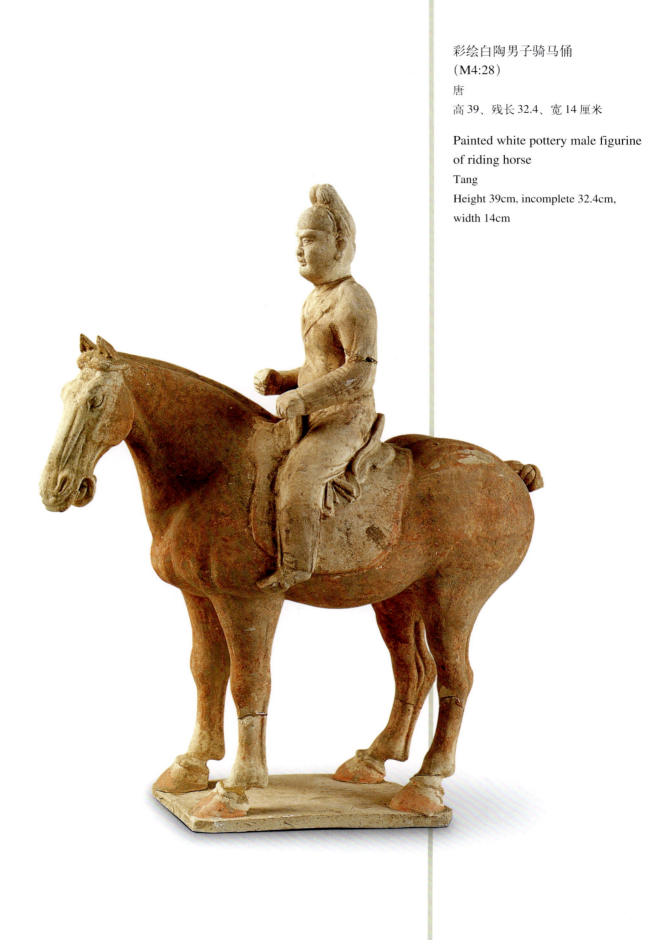

陶骑驼俑（M33:23）
唐
高 45、驼身长 32 厘米

Pottery figurine of riding camel
Tang
Height 45cm, length of camel 32cm

陶牛（M141:22）
唐
高 13、长 18.8 厘米

Pottery cattle
Tang
Height 13cm, length 18.8cm

铜镜（M160:1）
唐
直径 12 厘米

Bronze mirror
Tang
Diameter 12cm

白瓷执壶（M265:1）
宋
高 23.5、口径 11.5、底径 6.7 厘米

White porcelain pot with handle at the
side
Song
Height 23.5cm, rim diameter 11.5cm, base
diameter 6.7cm

青花瓷碗（M124:1）
明
高 4.8、口径 13、圈足径 5.3 厘米

Blue-and-white porcelain bowl
Ming
Height 4.8cm, rim diameter 13cm,
circular base diameter 5.3cm

关帝庙遗址
Guandimiao site

关帝庙遗址位于荥阳市豫龙镇关帝庙村西南部。2006年河南省文物考古研究所开始实施发掘，2007年继续发掘，两年累计发掘面积13300平方米。发现灰坑1100多个，灰沟11条，房基26座，墓葬200余座，水井18口，陶窑16座，祭祀坑13座。出土大批包括青铜、陶、石、骨、蚌、角、铁、瓷等质地在内的文化遗物。

关帝庙遗址发现了仰韶文化晚期、商代晚期、西周、东周、汉代、唐代、宋代、清代等时期的文化遗存，尤以商代晚期文化遗存最为丰富。商代晚期文化遗存内部有功能分区：居住遗址集中在遗址的中部偏北处（发掘区的西部），居住遗址中及其周围分布有生活用水井；制陶遗址和居住遗

陶鬲（H641:1）
商
高19、口径18厘米

Pottery Li
Shang
Height 19cm, rim diameter 18cm

陶鼎（H584:1）　商　高33、口径22.5厘米
Pottery Ding tripod　Shang　Height 33cm, rim diameter 22.5cm

址没有明显的分界，但陶窑周围有类似水窖的遗存；祭祀遗存比较集中分布在发掘区南部，有燎祭遗存和瘗埋遗迹；墓葬区两处，一处位于遗址东北部围沟之外，一处位于围沟之内，居住址西南；居住遗址与墓葬区之间，有沟相隔。

　　保存完整的商代晚期小型聚落的大面积接露，在商代考古发掘中尚属首次，对于探讨商代晚期的聚落结构、社会形态等，具有重要的意义。本次发掘充分利用现代科学技术，对地质地貌、动物、植物、人骨、石制品以及各类测试土样等考古信息进行全面采集，为聚落考古、古代环境复原、生业、人类行为等学术课题的综合研究构建了基础。

陶鬲（H412:1）
商
高 27、口径 26 厘米

Pottery Li
Shang
Height 27cm, rim diameter 26cm

The Guandimiao site is located in southwest Guandimiao village, Yulong town in Xingyang city. Henan Provincial Institute of Cultural Relics and Archaeology excavated the site in 2006 and 2007. The total excavation area is 13300 square meters. The excavation revealed more than 1100 pits, 11 ash ditches, 26 house foundations, over 200 tombs, 18 wells, 16 kilns, and 13 sacrificial pits. A large number of artifacts including bronze, pottery, stone, bone, shell, antler, iron, and porcelain categories were collected from the site. The remains recovered from the site cover the late Yangshao, late Shang, Western Zhou, Eastern Zhou, Han, Tang, Song and Qing periods. Of these, the Shang remains dominate the assemblage. The late Shang features can be divided into several functional areas: the habitation area is located in the mid-north part, and some wells were found around the area; there is no clear dividing line between the pottery-making area and the habitation area, but there are some features like water vaults around pottery kilns; the sacrificial features are distributed in the south of the excavation area; the burial area is located in the northeast of the site; there is a ditch between the habitation area and the burial area.

It is for the first time in the Shang archaeology that we revealed a well-preserved small late Shang settlement. The excavation is of importance for investigating the settlement pattern and social structure in the late Shang Dynasty. This fieldwork carefully collected environmental, faunal, floral, human, stone and various soil samples, which provide the important information for a study of settlement archaeology, environmental reconstruction, subsistence economy and human behavior.

陶鬲 （H478:1）
商
高 19、口径 17.5 厘米

Pottery Li
Shang
Height 19cm, rim diameter 17.5cm

鹿角（H627:2）
商
残长 54 厘米

Deer antler
Shang
Incomplete length 54cm

陶鬲（F20:1）
商
高 21、口径 20 厘米

Pottery Li
Shang
Height 21cm, rim diameter 20cm

陶簋（H41 ②:1）

商

高 21.5、口径 29、圈足径 17 厘米

Pottery Gui

Shang

Height 21.5cm, rim diameter 29cm, circular based diameter 17cm

铁岭墓地
Tieling cemetery

铁岭墓地位于新郑市东北部，西南距郑韩故城2.5公里，南北长650、东西宽600米，面积近40万平方米。2006年7月，郑州市文物考古研究院对该墓地进行了发掘，发掘面积3000平方米，发掘墓葬105座（除2座为明清墓外，余均为东周墓），龙山时期灰坑6个，西周早期灰坑18个，唐代灰坑5个。出土陶、泥、玉、水晶、铜、铁等一批精美文物。

铁岭墓地东周墓葬数量众多，可分为大、中、小型墓葬，大中型墓占多数，小型墓相对较少。墓葬大多为东西向，少量墓葬大致呈南北向，而且南北向的墓葬均位于墓地东部边缘。出土陶器组合的以大型墓葬为主，陶器的基本组合为鼎、鬲、罐、豆，鼎、豆、壶和鼎、豆、壶、盘、匜。中型墓几乎没有随葬陶器的，个别随葬有铜璜、铜带钩、铁带钩、

陶匜（M252:4）　春秋　高8.1、长15、宽8.7厘米
Pottery Yi　Sping and Autumn　Height 8.1cm, Length 15cm, Width 8.7cm

陶鼎（M252:2） 春秋 通高20.5、口径15厘米
Pottery Ding Tripod Spring and Autumn Height 20.5cm, Rim Diameter 15cm

水晶环之类。小型墓中的土洞墓中随葬有铜璜、铜带钩、铁带钩及陶罐。

龙山晚期的器物有罐、小口罐、瓮、双腹盆、罱、豆、豆盘、碗、器盖等；西周早期器物有鬲、罐、瓮、簋、盆、缸等；东周器物主要有鼎、豆、盖豆、壶、高柄壶、折肩罐、盘、匜、红陶鬲等。汉唐器物以瓮、盆、钵为主。

铁岭墓地系郑韩故城外围一处比较重要的东周墓地，它的发掘为郑韩墓葬的综合研究提供了重要资料。

陶鸟（M252:8）　Pottery bird
春秋　Spring and Autumn
高 3 厘米　Height 3cm

玛瑙环（M100:3）　Agate ring
战国　Warring States
直径 7.2、孔径 4.3 厘米　Diameter 7.2cm, orifice diameter 4.3cm

The Tieling cemetery is located in northeast Xinzheng city. It is about 40ha. in area, 650m long in north-south direction, and 600m wide in west-east direction. Zhengzhou Municipal Institute of Cultural Relics and Archaeology excavated the cemetery in July 2006. The excavation area is 3000 square meters. The excavation revealed 105 tombs and 29 pits, and unearthed pottery, mud, jade, crystal, bronze and iron artifacts.

The large number of Eastern Zhou tombs can be divided into large, medium and small categories. Most of them are large and medium tombs buried in west-east direction. The large tombs unearthed a number of pottery vessels. The basic compositions are a Ding tripod, a Li, a jar and a Dou, a Ding tripod, a Dou and a pot, as well as a Ding tripod, a Dou, a pot and a dish. The offering objects from the medium tombs are very few. Some of medium tombs unearthed bronze Huang, bronze belt hooks, iron belt hooks and crystal rings. The small cavity-chambered tombs unearthed bronze Huang, bronze belt hooks, iron belt hooks and pottery jars.

The artifacts recovered from the Longshan deposits are jars, small-orifice jars, urns, double-belly basins, Dou, dishes, bowls, and lids, from the early Western Zhou deposits are Li, jars. urns, Gui, and basins, and from the Eastern Zhou deposits are Ding, Dou, pots, high-handle pots, shoulder-folded jars, dishes, red pottery and Li, urns, basins and bowls dominate the artifact assemblage of Han and Tang.

The Tieling cemetery is an important Eastern Zhou cemetery outside the Zheng and Han ancient city. The excavation provides important materials for a synthetic study of Zheng and Han tombs.

玉环（左：M99:13、右：M99:16）
战国
左：直径4.1、孔径2.45厘米
右：直径2.85、孔径1.5厘米
Jade Ring
Warring states
Left:　Diameter 4.1cm,
　　　orifice diameter 2.45cm
Right: Diameter 2.85cm,
　　　orifice diameter 1.5cm

海贝（M229:13）
战国
长2.5、宽2、厚1.2厘米
Seashell
Warring states
Length 2.5cm, width 2cm,
depth 1.2cm

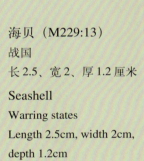

三彩钵（H24:1）
唐
高11.5、口径7.6厘米
Tricolor bowal
Tang
Height 11.5cm, rim diameter 7.6cm

铜鼎（M222:1）　春秋晚期－战国早期　高29.1、口径23.7厘米
Bronze Ding tripod　Late Spring and Autumn to early Warring States　Height 29.1cm, rim diameter 23.7cm

胡庄墓地位于新郑市"郑韩故城"之西，是郑韩故城外围的重要墓地之一。2006 年河南省文物考古研究所开始发掘，至 2007 年底，揭露面积 12000 多平方米，共清理中小型东周墓葬 330 座，其中春秋墓葬 35 座，战国墓葬 276 座，时代不明的墓葬 6 座。出土青铜、铁、玉、骨、陶等各种文物 500 余件，其中有鼎、敦、舟，鼎、敦、盘、舟、匜等青铜礼器 9 件；戈、矛、玉鞘短剑、镞等青铜兵器 8 件，以玉鞘铜短剑最为珍贵；镜、管、扣、带勾、璜、马衔、车軎等青铜杂器 110 余件；圭、璜、饼、环、珠等玉器 94 件；玛瑙环 9 件；水晶环及带钩、镢等铁器 7 件；珠、管、贝、扳指、带钩等骨器 35 件；鬲、盂、豆、罐、盖豆、鼎、壶、钵、碗、盘、舟、匜、盆、罍等陶器 190 件。

胡庄墓地是以两座带封土的战国晚期韩国王陵级大墓为主的大片墓地，两座大墓东西并列，规模宏大，形制特殊，国内罕见。大墓周围发现 3 条近长方形环壕，壕沟间距在 20 米左右，内壕和中壕近长方形，外壕近长条形椭圆形环状，这种布局国内也只在东周时期陕西秦公陵园有所发现。外壕南北长约 237、东西宽约 220 米，壕内面积达 50000 平方米左右，组成了由两座"中"字形大墓，"中"字形封土，"中"字形封土上建筑，1 座拐角形墓旁建筑，3 条环壕组成的陵园形态，填补了东周列国王侯陵墓和韩国陵园形态的发现空白，是目前为止最为重要的发现。

M2 封土上陵寝建筑保存较好，由散水、壁洞、柱石和部分屋顶瓦砾层等组成。这种建筑形态是此前商周时期高级贵族墓上平地建筑转变到秦始皇陵封土以外设便殿的过渡形态。在墓室壁和墓道底部发现大面积的白灰和朱砂装饰痕，填土中发现版筑痕、木网木棍灰痕和疑似房顶的木板灰层等。

在西北发掘区的北端发现 1 条东西向的战国道路，宽 7 米左右，由路面和路边沟组成，路面上有多道车辙痕迹，是郑韩故城外围发现的首条大道，为研究韩都交通提供了重要新材料。

铜带钩（M53:3） 战国 长 12.8、宽 2 厘米
Bronze belt hook　Warring States　Length 12.8cm, width 2cm

铜匜（M47:2）
春秋晚期－战国早期
高10.1、长22.6、宽10.7厘米

Bronze Yi
Late Spring and Autumn to early Warring States
Height 10.1cm, length 22.6cm, width 10.7cm

The Huzhuang cemetery, one of the important cemeteries outside the Ancient Zheng and Han City, is located in the west of Ancient Zheng and Han City. Henan Provincial Institute of Cultural Relics and Archaeology have excavated the cemetery since 2006. The excavation area was 12000 square meters by the end of 2007. The excavation revealed 330 medium and small tombs dating to the Eastern Zhou, and unearthed more than 500 various artifacts including bronze, iron, jade, bone, and pottery categories.

There are two large tombs with grave mound dating to the late Warring States in the Huzhuang cemetery. They may have been the king-class tombs of the Han State. The two tombs parallel with one in the east and one in the west. Three approximately rectangular looped ditches, inner, middle and outer, were found around them. The distance between ditches is about 20m. This kind of layout was only found at King Qin cemetery of the Qin State in Shaanxi. The outer ditch is 237m long in north-south direction, 220m wide in west-east direction, and 5 ha in area. So, the cemetery is composed of two large " 中 "shaped tombs with " 中 "shaped grave mounds, buildings on the "中"shaped grave mounds, one building on the side of tombs, and three looped ditches. It fills in the gap in understanding of king-classed mausoleums in the Eastern Zhou and the cemetery pattern of Han State.

The building on the mound of M2 is well preserved. It is composed of drainage network, wall holes, post stones, and layers of roof tiles. A large area of lime and cinnabar remains were found on chamber walls and the bottom of tomb passage, and the marks of plate, crabstick, and possible ash layer of roof plates were found in the filling deposits.

A road with 7m wide and in west-east direction was revealed in the northern end of the northwest excavation part. It consists of road and roadside ditch. There are many tracks of on the road. This is the first road found outside the ancient Zheng and Han city, and provides new data for investigating the transportation in the Han capital.

铜舟（M219:1）
春秋晚期－战国早期
高9、口长径17.1、口短径9.9厘米

Bronze boat
Late Spring and Autumn to early Warring States
Height 9cm, rim long diameter 17.1cm, rim short diameter 9.9cm

陶罍（M302:12）　　　Pottery Lei
春秋　　　　　　　　Spring and Autumn
高 31、口径 14.6 厘米　Height 31cm, rim diameter 14.6cm

铜甗（M222:3）　　　　　　Bronze Yan
春秋晚期－战国早期　　　Late Spring and Autumn to early Warring States
高 37.5、釜口径 23.8、　　Height 37.5cm, rim diameter of Fu 23.8cm, base
釜底径 9.8、鬲口径 9 厘米　diameter of Fu 9.8cm, rim diameter of Li 9cm

铜敦（M222:2）

春秋晚期－战国早期

通高 18.1、口径 20.3 厘米

Bronze Dun

Late Spring and Autumn to early Warring States

Height 18.1cm, rim diameter 20.3cm

铜方壶（M222:4）
春秋晚期－战国早期
高 22.1、口长 9.3、口宽 5.75、
底长 8.5、底宽 5.7 厘米

Bronze rectangular pot
Late Spring and Autumn to early Warring States
Height 22.1cm, rim diameter 9.3cm, rim width 5.75cm,
base diameter length 8.5cm, base width 5.7cm

铜盘（M47:1）
春秋晚期－战国早期
高 7.4、口径 32.5 厘米

Bronze Pan
Late Spring and Autumn to early Warring States
Height 7.4cm, rim diameter 32.5cm

玉鞘和铜匕（M96 棺室:31）
春秋
玉鞘长 23.3、宽 7.4 厘米；
铜匕长 20.3、宽 2.6 厘米

Jade sheath and bronze dagger
Spring and Autumn
Length of jade sheath 23.3cm, width 7.4cm; length of bronze dagger
20.3cm, width 2.6cm

许昌

阳翟故城

Yangdi city-site

阳翟故城遗址，位于禹州市钧台办事处八里营村南，南水北调工程中线干渠332公里处。2006年6月武汉大学考古系进驻工地，开始了该项目的发掘和研究工作，至2007年底，共计发掘面积8000平方米。共清理西周、东周、汉、六朝及金元时期各类遗迹1116处，其中包括道路4条，夯土基址2处，陶窑4座，沟12条，灶28个，井29眼，墓葬24座，灰坑913个。共出土瓷、陶、釉陶、玻璃、铜、铁、骨、石器等各类完整或能复原的遗物2286件，包括铜钱193枚，骰子52枚，围棋子126枚，瓷器等。器物类型有碗、钵、盆、盘、碟、杯、盏、罐、釜、瓶、擂钵、器盖、簪、梳子、砚、灯、针、枕（残片）、纺轮、瓦、镞、俑、骰子、围棋子、象棋子、石球、钱币等。

瓷器出土的数量最多，器物类型有碗、钵、盆、盘、碟、杯、盏、罐、瓶、器盖、枕（残片）、人俑、动物俑（马、蛙、鸭）、围棋子等。瓷器以白瓷、黑瓷为主，还出土了一件极为少见的钧瓷梅瓶。

从发掘所获情况看，该遗址未发现夯土痕迹，根据发现的两周时期的少量遗存和一小片周代墓地来分析，南水北调中线工程总干渠应是在两周堆积的南部边缘地带穿过，韩国都城阳翟故城城址均不在干渠占压范围内。阳翟故城遗址出土了一大批金元时期的遗迹、遗物，表明遗址为一处不多见的金元时期普通平民的生活遗址，对于了解金元时期一般民众的社会生活状况非常有价值。

The Yangdi ancient city is located in the south of Baliying village, Juntai town in Yuzhou city. The Archaeology Department of Wuhan University excavated the site in 2006 and 2007. A total of 8000 square meters was excavated. The excavation revealed 1116 features, including 4 roads, 2 rammed foundations, 4 pottery kilns, 12 ditches, 28 stoves, 29 wells, 24 tombs, and 913 pits. A total of 2286 artifacts were recovered from the site involved in porcelain, pottery, glazed pottery, glass, bronze, iron, bone, and stone objects.

The majority of the artifacts are porcelain vessels including bowls, Bo, basins, dishes, cups, jars, vases, lids, pillows, human figurines, animal figurines (horse, frog, and duck) and pieces of I-go. White and black glazed porcelain vessels dominate the porcelain assemblage.

The excavation at the Yangdi ancient city site did not reveal any rammed feature, suggesting that the central area of the ancient city site is not in the excavation area. The large number of features and artifacts dating to Jin and Yuan, indicates that the site is a common settlement in the Jin and Yuan periods. It is of importance for understanding the social living of civilian in the Jin and Yuan periods.

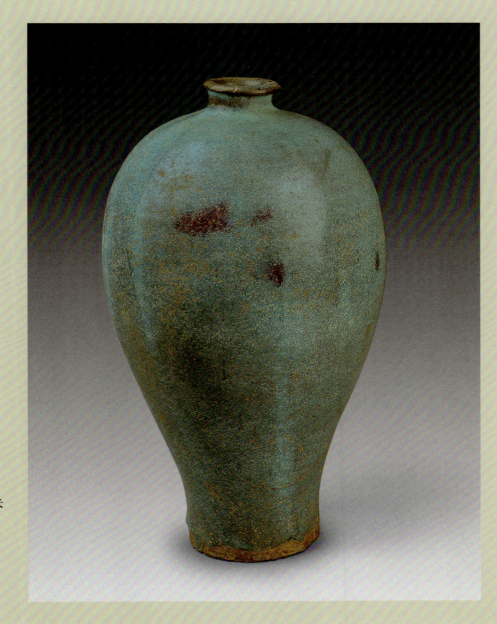

梅瓶（M1:5）
元
高33、口径5.2、底径9.2厘米

Prunus vase
Yuan
Height 33cm, rim diameter 5.2cm,
base diameter 9.2cm

崔张汉墓群
Cuizhang Han cemetery

崔张汉墓群位于禹州市梁北镇三峰山东峰（新峰山）山坡的台地上。北距禹州市区约5000米，东南距崔张村不足300米，南距张得乡约4000米。

2006年4月，河南省文物考古研究所、许昌市文物工作队、禹州市文物工作队联合组成考古队，对其进行抢救性的考古发掘，共发掘墓葬60座，除2座清代墓外，其余均为汉墓。汉代墓葬分土坑竖穴和洞室两大类，其中土坑竖穴墓7座，洞室墓51座。由于多数墓葬严重被盗，葬具葬式多不详，残存有骨架的，葬式有仰身直肢和侧身直肢两种，随葬品多寡不一。

出土随葬品共206件。其中陶器127件（组），器形有罐、壶、盆、奁、耳杯、纺轮、磨、碓、灶、甑、井、熏炉、猪圈、猪、狗等；瓷器2件（清代墓出土），皆为双系瓷罐；铜器38件，有镜、带钩、刀、印章、车軎、环、剑鞘、撮斗等；铁器11件，有剑、削、刀、盏、饰件等；骨器11件，有蝉、鼻塞、耳塞等；玉器4件，有环、印章、片等；石器饰品1件；蚌器饰品1件；杂器11件。另有铜钱700余枚，铁钱2枚。

崔张汉墓群尽管多数墓葬被

铜兽（M39:2）
汉
高5.4厘米

Bronze animal
Han
Height 5.4cm

铜镜（M24:6） 汉 直径14厘米
Bronze mirror Han Diameter 14cm

盗，但还是遗留下了较为丰富的文化遗物，80%的墓葬有随葬品，随葬陶器1～11件不等，以罐、壶、盆或奁或耳杯组合为多。据出土物推断，发掘的这58座汉墓的时期为西汉晚期到东汉晚期。

崔张汉墓群多为洞室结构的墓葬，这种形制的墓葬在此次崔张汉墓发掘区分布面积之广、数量之多，在禹州地区的考古发掘中尚不多见，为研究中原地区汉代的社会生产、社会生活以及葬制、葬俗等方面提供了翔实的实物资料。

铜镜（M46:12）
汉
直径 10 厘米

Bronze mirror
Han
Diameter 10cm

The Cuizhang Han cemetery is located in the hillside of Dongfeng Mountain, Liangbei town in Yuzhou city. Henan Provincial Institute of Cultural Relics and Archaeology, Xuchang Municipal Team of Archaeology, and Yuzhou Municipal Team of Archaeology excavated the cemetery in April 2006, and revealed 60 tombs, of which 58 are Han tombs. Han tombs can be divided into shaft and cavity-chambered categories. Of these, seven are shaft tombs and 51 are cavity-chambered tombs. A total of 206 offering objects were recovered from the tombs. Of these, 127 are pottery vessels including jars, pots, basins, Lian, cups, spin wheels, millings, pestles, stoves, Zeng, wells, incense burners, sties, pigs, and dogs. Although most of the tombs at the Cuizhang cemetery were looted, 80% burials unearthed offering objects. The artifacts indicate that 58 Han tombs date to the period between the late Western Han and the late Eastern Han.

The majority of the Cuizhang burials are cavity-chambered tombs. It is for the first time that we find so many cavity-chambered tombs in Yuzhou region. The excavation provides rich materials for investigating the social production, and subsistence, as well as the burial system and custom in the Han Dynasty in the Central Plain.

铜镜（M18:12）　　　Bronze mirror
汉　　　　　　　　　Han
直径 14.1 厘米　　　 Diameter 14.1cm

新峰汉墓群
Xinfeng Han cemetery

　　新峰汉墓群位于禹州市梁北镇境内，北距禹州市区约5公里，跨梁北镇苏王口村和郭村两个行政村。古墓群处于东峰山东坡北端的梯级台地上南北长约600、东西宽220米，面积132000平方米。

　　2007年6月，河南文物考古研究所、许昌市文物工作队、禹

陶鼎（M18:2）　汉　通高17、口径13.8厘米
Pottery Ding tripod　Han　Height 17cm, rim diameter 13.8cm

陶灶（M3:5） 汉 长19、宽15.8、高10.9厘米
Pottery stove Han Length 19cm, width 15.8cm, height 10.9cm

州市文物工作队联合组成考古队，对新峰墓地进行抢救性发掘。共发掘面积4100平方米，清理古墓葬174座，其中汉墓164座，唐墓3座，宋墓6座，明墓1座。墓葬分土坑竖穴墓和洞室墓两大类，其中土坑竖穴墓85座，洞室墓99座。排列无规律，葬式有仰身直肢、侧身直肢和侧身曲肢葬三种。

随葬品多寡不一。器物类型有鼎、壶、罐、盒、盆、碗、樽、熏炉、案、耳杯、灶、钵、釜、甑、磨、纺轮等。其中有一部分为釉陶器。组合有鼎、壶、盒、罐，鼎、壶、盆或壶、豆、盘等。其他随葬品还有铜镜、铜带钩、铜铃、车马饰件、铁剑、铁削、铅印章、玉口、玉塞、石砚、骨质品等。

新峰墓地尽管多数墓葬被盗，但还是遗留下了较为丰富的文化遗物，根据墓葬形制及出土随葬品综合分析，发掘的这164座汉代墓葬的时代初步确定为西汉早期至东汉中晚期。新峰墓地的发掘，为研究中原地区汉代人口的地域分布、生产活动及埋葬习俗等提供了实物资料。

陶壶(M10:76)
汉
通高 50、口径 18、足径 16 厘米

Pottery pot
Han
Height 50cm, rim diameter 18cm, base diameter 16cm

The Xinfeng Han cemetery is located in Liangbei town, Yuzhou city. It is 13.2 ha. in area, 600 m long in north-south direction and 220m wide in west-east direction. Henan Provincial Institute of Cultural Relics and Archaeology, Xuchang Municipal Team of Archaeology, and Yuzhou Municipal Team of Archaeology excavated the cemetery in June of 2006, and revealed 174 tombs in 4100 square meters. These tombs include 164 Han tombs, 3 Tang tombs, 6 Song tombs and one Ming tomb. These tombs can be divided into two categories, shaft tombs and cavity-chambered tombs. Of these, there are 85 shaft tombs and 99 cavity-chambered tombs. The burial manners include extended, sideways extended, and sideways flexed burials. The funeral objects are Ding tripods, pots, jars, boxes, basins, bowls, Zun, incense burners, tables, cups, stoves, kettles, Zeng, millings, and spin wheels. The compositions include a Ding tripod, a pot, a box and a jar, as well as a Ding tripod, a pot and a basin or a pot, a Dou, a dish. Other funeral objects are bronze mirrors, bronze belt hooks, bronze bells, bronze chariot and harness ornaments, iron swords, iron knives, lead seals, jade mouths, jade stuff, stone inkstones, and bone artifacts.

Based on the burial structure and the characteristic of funeral objects, these 164 Han tombs can be dated to the period between the early Western Han and the mid-late Eastern Han. The excavation at the Xinfeng cemetery provides materials for investigating the population distribution, production activity and burial custom in the Han Dynasty in the Central Plain.

平顶山

◎ 文集遗址

文集遗址
Wenji site

文集遗址位于叶县常村乡文集自然村西南地，为县级文物保护单位。2006~2007年河南省文物考古研究所对该遗址进行了发掘，发掘面积为10400平方米，清理遗迹619处，包括房基26处，水井4口，地灶50个，窖藏坑23个，灰坑483个，灰沟17条，灰池17个等。

遗址出土器物按质地可分为陶、瓷、三彩、铁、铜、石等六大类。瓷器可以分为白瓷、黑瓷、青瓷三种，器形有碗、盘、钵、盅、瓶、盂、器盖、灯、执壶、注子、盏、尊、盆、缸等。陶器有缸、盆、罐、砚台、龟、砖、瓦、兽吻等，白陶器有围棋子、骰子、弹丸等。三彩器有枕、灯等。铁器有犁铧、罐等。铜器有镜、钱币、人形饰等。石器有磨、柱础、砚台等。

该遗址的窖藏坑年代均在金末元初，并出土了基本完好的钧瓷、青瓷与白瓷器等30余件，尤其是一套完整的配有盏

钧瓷茶盏（H444:1~3）
金
通高8.05、盖口径8.4、
杯口径7.4、盘口径11.5厘米

Tea cup, Jun ware
Jin
Height 8.05cm, rim diameter of lid
8.4cm, rim diameter of cup 7.4cm,
rim diameter of dish 11.5cm

红绿彩执镜女俑
（H487:65）
金
高 13.2 厘米

Red and green glazed female
figurine with holding mirror
Jin
Height 13.2cm

白底黑花执扇女俑
（T1307 ②:1）
金
高 11 厘米

White glazed female figurine with
holding fan in black floral design
Jin
Height 11cm

托、盏碗与盏盖的茶盏极具艺
术价值。

文集遗址是一处较大规模的
民间集镇遗址，为研究中原地区
平顶山一带唐、宋、金、元时期的
历史文化面貌提供了一大批珍贵
的资料，也有助于研究金元时期
民间的经济贸易往来与相互交流，
同时为金元瓷器的分期研究提供
了珍贵资料。

三彩枕 （H487:1）　　　　Tricolor pillow
金　　　　　　　　　　　Jin
长 52.7、宽 21、高 14.2 厘米　　Length 52.7cm, width 21cm, height 14.2cm

The Wenji site is located in southwest Wenji village, Changcun town in Yexian, Pingdingshan city. Henan Provincial Institute of Cultural Relics and Archaeology excavated the site in 2006 and 2007. The excavation area is 10400 square meters. The excavation revealed 619 features including 26 house foundations, 4 wells, 50 earth stoves, 23 storage containers, 483 ash pits, 17 ash ditches, and 17 ash ponds.

The unearthed artifacts can be classified into pottery, porcelain, tricolor pottery, iron, bronze and stone categories. Porcelain glazes include white, black and celadon categories. Porcelain vessels have bowls, dishes, Bo, cups, vases, Yu, lids, lamps, pots, Zhan, Zun, basins, and urns. Pottery vessels include urns, basins, jars, inkstone, tortoises, bricks, tiles, and beast mouths. White pottery artifacts witness white and black pieces of I-go, dices, and pills. Tricolor pottery artifacts include pillows and lamps. Iron artifacts have ploughshares and jars. Bronzes ob-

jects witness mirrors, coins, and human-shaped ornaments. Stone artifacts include millings, post foundations, and inkstones.

The storages, dating to the end of Jin and the beginning of Yuan, unearthed more than 30 well-preserved porcelain vessels of Jun ware, celadon and white porcelain vessels. In particular, a complete set of tea vessel with a cup saucer, a bowl and a lid possesses artistic value.

The Wenji site is a large site of civil market town. The excavation provides important data for investigating the historical situation during the Tang, Song, Jin and Yuan periods in Pingdingshan region, the civil economic exchange in the Jin and Yuan periods, and the periodization of Jin and Yuan porcelain.

青瓷碗（H444:10）
金
高 5.7、口径 13.6、底径 3.8 厘米

Celadon bowl
Jin
Height 5.7cm, rim diameter 13.6cm, base diameter 3.8cm

青瓷碗（H463:1）
金
高 5、口径 10.8、
底径 3.2 厘米

Celadon bowl
Jin
Height 5cm, rim diameter 10.8cm,
base diameter 3.2cm

青瓷碗（H444:11）
金
高 6.1、口径 13、底径 3.4 厘米

Celadon bowl
Jin
Height 6.1cm, rim diameter 13cm,
base diameter 3.4cm

青瓷碗（H444:12）
金
高 5.4、口径 13.9、
底径 4.8 厘米

Celadon bowl
Jin
Height 5.4cm, rim diameter 13.9cm,
base diameter 4.8cm

青瓷碗（F27:18）
金
高 5.45、口径 12.2、底径 4.5 厘米

Celadon bowl
Jin
Height 5.45cm, rim diameter 12.2cm, base diameter 4.5cm

青瓷盘（H281:1）
金
高 2.5、口径 20.4、底径 12.6 厘米

Celadon dish
Jin
Height 2.5cm, rim diameter 20.4cm,
base diameter 12.6cm

青瓷盘（H444:9）
金
高 5、口径 23.8、底径 13.6 厘米

Celadon dish
Jin
Height 5cm, rim diameter 23.8cm,
base diameter 13.6cm

青瓷盏托（T1608 ② b:1）
金
高 2.65、口径 12、底径 5.3 厘米

Celadon cup saucer
Jin
Height 2.65cm, rim diameter 12cm, base diameter 5.3cm

钧瓷碗（H105:1）
金
高 8.3、口径 19.8、底径 6.1 厘米

Porcelain bowl, Jun ware
Jin
Height 8.3cm, rim diameter 19.8cm, base diameter 6.1cm

钧瓷盘 （H444:7）
金
高 3.4、口径 16.5、
底径 5.5 厘米

Porcelain dish, Jun ware
Jin
Height 3.4cm, rim diameter 16.5cm,
base diameter 5.5cm

瓷花口瓶盖 （H444:6）
金
高 6.5、直径 6.7 厘米

Porcelain vase lid with lace rim
Jin
Height 6.5cm, diameter 6.7cm

白底黑花瓷碗 （H95:1）
金
高 7.75、口径 11.5、底径 6.2 厘米

White glazed bowl with floral design in black
Jin
Height 7.75cm, rim diameter 11.5cm, base diameter 6.2cm

红绿彩碗（H656:1）
金
高 5.5、口径 15.5、底径 5.5 厘米

Red and green glazed bowl
Jin
Height 5.5cm, rim diameter 15.5cm,
base diameter 5.5cm

瓜棱白瓷盂（T1707 ② F:1）
金
高 7.1、口径 9.8、底径 5.7 厘米

White glazed cup with melon-shaped design
Jin
Height 7.1cm, rim diameter 9.8cm, base diameter 5.7cm

白瓷褐点纹灯（T1607 ② F:1）
金
高 6.6、口径 9.6、底径 4.4 厘米

White glazed lamp with brown
dotted design
Jin
Height 6.6cm, rim diameter 9.6cm,
base diameter 4.4cm

黑釉折沿瓷碗（H375:1）
金
高 4.7、口径 13.5、
底径 3.55 厘米

Black glazed bowl with
folded brim
Jin
Height 4.7cm, rim diameter
13.5cm, base diameter 3.55cm

白底黑花瓷碗（T1:1）
元
高 13.3、口径 26、底径 8.4 厘米

White glazed bowl with floral
design in black
Yuan
Height 13.3cm, rim diameter 26cm,
base diameter 8.4cm

白底黑花瓷盆（H487:1）

元

高 10.03、口径 38.5、底径 24 厘米

White glazed basin with floral
design in black

Yuan

Height 10.03cm, rim diameter 38.5cm,
base diameter 24cm

白底黑花瓷盆（H214:5）
元
高 15.4、口径 31.5、底径 20 厘米

White glazed basin with floral
design in black
Yuan
Height 15.4cm, rim diameter 31.5cm,
base diameter 20cm

白底黑花"霄"字瓷盘（H814:1）

元

高4.3、口径16.7、底径5.7厘米

White glazed dish with word
"Xiao" and floral design in black

Yuan

Height 4.3cm, rim diameter 16.7cm,
base diameter 5.7cm

白底黑花瓷盘（H66:1）
元
高4、口径14.8、底径5.9厘米

White glazed dish with floral
design in black
Yuan
Height 4cm, rim diameter 14.8cm,
base 5.9cm

铜镜（H22:3）
金
直径8.8厘米

Bronze mirror
Jin
Diameter 8.8cm

铜镜（H487:69）
元
直径6.9厘米

Bronze mirror
Yuan
Diameter 6.9cm

南阳

◎ 徐家岭楚墓群

◎ 东沟长岭楚墓群

前田洼遗址
Qiantianwa site

前田洼遗址位于南阳市北京大道与312国道交叉口东南角，正南距全国重点文物保护单位武侯祠约6公里。2006年6~9月，河南省文物考古研究所、南阳市文物考古研究所对前田洼遗址进行了钻探和发掘，发掘面积1050平方米，清理汉代和清代墓葬34座，灰坑1个，灰沟1条，出土文物200余件，取得了初步考古成果。

汉代墓葬20座，均为中小型砖室墓，根据形制可分为长方形单室、并列双室、前后室墓，刀把形墓，"甲"字形墓。墓葬均被盗扰，出土随葬器物不能全部代表该墓地的器物组合，所出器物主要有陶瓮、陶罐、陶壶、陶豆、陶奁盒、陶盒、陶井、陶灶、陶勺、陶案、陶盘、陶耳杯、陶碓、陶猪圈、陶狗、陶鸡、陶俑等及五铢钱。陶器以红陶为主，灰陶次之，红釉陶占多数。这批汉代墓葬以东汉晚期墓居多，这对南阳汉墓的分期提供了重要资料，具有较高的研究价值。

清代墓葬14座，均为小型土坑竖穴墓，可分为长方形单室或双室墓、梯形墓、"凸"字形墓、刀把形墓四种形制。有单人葬和合葬墓。其中8座清代墓，上下有序、年代有别，应为一家族墓地。随葬品不多，个别随葬简单的铜饰或少量银饰，部分墓的头端棺外中间下部仅置放小瓷罐，多数死者的头骨下横枕板瓦。

银簪（M12:7）
清
长9厘米

Silver hairpin
Qing
Length 9cm

银头饰（M12:5）
清
长 14.7、宽 2.1 厘米

Silver headgear
Qing
Length 14.7cm, width 2.1cm

The Qiantianwa site is located in Nanyang city. Henan Provincial Institute of Cultural Relics and Archaeology, and Nanyang Municipal Institute of Cultural Relics and Archaeology excavated the site from June to September of 2006. The excavation area is 1050 square meters. The excavation revealed 34 Han and Qing tombs, one pit, and one ash ditch, and collected more than 200 artifacts.

The 20 Han tombs are all medium and small brick-chambered tombs, which can be divided into rectangular single-chamber tomb, double-chamber tomb, hilt-shaped tomb, and Chinese word "甲" shaped tomb. All of the tombs were looted, so the unearthed artifacts cannot represent the composition of offering objects. The unearthed articles mainly include pottery urns, jars, pots, Dou, Lianhe, boxes, wells, stoves, scoops, tables, dishes, cups, pestles, sties, dogs, chickens, figurines, and Wuzhu coins. The late Eastern Han tombs dominate the burial assemblage, and provide important data for investigating the periodization of Han tombs in Nanyang.

Fourteen tombs are small shaft tombs dating to the Qing Dynasty. They can be classified into rectangular single-cambered or double-chambered tomb, trapezoid tomb, "凸" shaped tomb, and hilt-shaped tomb. There are single burials and joint burials. Of these, eight tombs were arranged in age order, suggesting that they should belong to a family cemetery. The offering objects are few. Some tombs unearthed bronze or silver ornaments.

徐家岭楚墓群
Xujialing Chu cemetery

徐家岭墓地位于淅川县西南约47公里的仓房镇沿江村郭家窑小组东南，属丹江水库蓄水前丹江西岸的丘陵，地势由东向西渐高。海拔高度155~167米。2006年11月3日~2007年1月23日河南省文物考古研究所与南阳市文物考古研究所对徐家岭被盗的3座墓葬进行了抢救性发掘。

M11为一座"甲"字形墓，全长19.7米，方向90°。墓道位于东部，现存8级台阶。墓道口长8.2、宽2.7~3.2米。墓室平面长方形，墓口长11.5、宽10米，墓底长6.25、宽6米，墓室深10.5米。墓口至墓底有三级生土台阶。墓室底部四周有熟土二层台。墓室的棺椁已经腐朽，一椁重棺。椁为长方形，长4.4、宽3.7米。椁室中部偏北置一外棺。外棺长2.2、宽1.6米。内棺长1.85、宽0.6米。墓主人头向东，仰身直肢，双手交

小口铜鼎（M11:11）
春秋
通高44.5、口径23厘米

Bronze Ding tripod with small orifice
Spring and Autumn
Height 44.5cm, rim diameter 23cm

铜车軎
(M11:108、109)
战国
长 6.5 厘米

Bronze Wei
(the endpiece of axle)
Warring States
Length 6.5cm

又放于下腹部。棺内放置有葬玉和佩玉。棺下有一长方形腰坑，坑内有腐朽的狗骨。北边厢和西边厢内各置一棺，两棺内各有一具人骨架。墓室底部东西端各有条南北向的垫木槽。M11虽有两个盗洞，但大部分基本保存完好。器物主要放置在南、东边厢。铜器95件，按用途可分为礼器、乐器、车马器、兵器等。礼器有鼎5件，簠3件，敦3件，壶2件，及尊缶、小口鼎、瓶、盂、浴缶、勺、盘、匜等。乐器有纽钟一组11件。车马器有车軎、马衔、合页等。兵器有戈、矛等。玉石器主要有石磬1组13件及玉璧、环、珩、牌等。另有陶豆、罐、角质杯等。时代为战国早期，墓主人为大夫级贵族，女性。

M12墓口近方形。土坑竖穴木椁墓。墓口长7、宽6.3~6.5米；墓底长4.9、宽3.62、深7米。葬具已朽，从朽痕看为一椁一棺。椁室长3.6、宽2.8米。棺位于椁室中部偏西处。墓主人仰身直肢，双手交叉放于腹部。该墓被严重盗扰，残存铜鼎、浴缶、盘、匜等。时代为春秋晚期偏晚。

M13 长方形土坑竖穴木椁墓。墓口长3.1、宽1.8、深2米。墓底四周有熟土二层台。一椁一棺。随葬品全为陶器，主要有鼎、敦、豆、壶、盉、盘、匜等。时代为战国中期。

本次发掘的M11是目前在南水北调中线工程中发现等级最高、保存比较完整且出土文物较多的一座大型楚墓葬。在小口鼎的铭文中使用了岁星纪年和太岁纪年两种纪年方法，推定该器铸造年代为公元前507年，为楚墓中此类鼎提供了断代依据，并且为春秋战国之际历法用岁星纪年提供了坚实的证据，对我国古代天文历法研究具有重要学术意义。

玉璜 （M11:28）
战国
长 14、宽 2.8、厚 0.35 厘米

Jade Huang
Warring States
Length 14cm, width 2.8cm, thickness 0.35cm

The Xujialing cemetery is located in Guojiayao, Cangfang town in Xichuan county. Henan Provincial Institute of Cultural Relics and Archaeology and Nanyang Municipal Institute of Cultural Relics and Archaeology excavated three tombs at the cemetery from November of 2006 to January of 2007.

M11 is a "甲" shaped tomb with 19.7m long and 90° in direction. The tomb passage is 8.2m long and 2.7-3.2m wide. The plan of the tomb is rectangular. The tomb mouth is 11.5m long and 10m wide, and the bottom is 6.25m long and 6m wide. The chamber is 10.5m in depth. There are three steps of local earth from tomb mouth to bottom. Around the bottom witnesses the secondary platform made of mottled earth. The two coffins and an outer coffin were moldered. The

outer coffin is rectangular with 4.4m long and 3.7m wide. One coffin is 2.2m long and 1.6m wide and the other coffin is 1.85m long and 0.6m wide. The occupant of the tomb heads to east with extended burial and double crossed hands being put on lower belly. Some jades were arranged in coffins. Under one coffin is a rectangular waist pit in which a moldered dog skeleton is observed. Two coffins were put in north and west of the chamber. Two human skeletons were observed in each coffin. Most of the offering objects were well preserved. The offering objects were mainly arranged in the south and east of the tomb. Ninety-five bronze vessels can be classified into ritual, musical instrument, chariot and harness ornament, and weapon categories. The tomb dates to the early Warring States. The occupant of the tomb is a female noble.

M12 is a rectangular shaft tomb with one inner coffin and one outer coffin. The tomb mouth is 7m long and 6.3-6.5m wide, and the bottom is 4.9m long and 3.62m wide. It is 7m in depth. The outer coffin is 3.6m long and 2.8m wide. The occupant of the tomb is extended burial with double crossed hands being put on the belly. The tomb was heavily disturbed and only remained a few objects. The tomb dates to the late Spring and Autumn period.

M13 is a rectangular shaft tomb with one inner coffin and one outer coffin. It is 3.1m long, 1.8m wide and 2m deep. Around the bottom witnesses the secondary platform made of mottled earth.

All of the funeral objects are pottery vessels including Ding tripod, Dun, Dou, pot, dish and so on. The tomb dates to the middle Warring States period.

M11 is a well-preserved large Chu tomb. The two annals methods of Suixing and Taisui were observed by inscriptions on a Ding tripod with small orifice, indicating that the Ding tripod was made in 507 BC. This Ding tripod provides the evidence of periodization for such kind of vessels recovered from Chu tombs, and the evidence of using the method of Suixing annals on the occasion of the Spring and Autumn and Warring States periods. It is of academic importance for chronometer and calendar research.

玉璧 （M11:69）
战国
直径 11、孔径 5.1、厚 0.7 厘米

Jade Bi
Warring States
Diameter 11cm, orifice diameter 5.1cm,
thickness 0.7cm

铜鼎（M11:18）
战国
通高 40.4、口径 38.2 厘米

Bronze Ding tripod
Warring States
Height 40.4cm, rim diameter 38.2cm

铜簠（M11:97）

战国

通高 22.4、长 33.2、宽 21.8 厘米

Bronze Fu

Warring States

Height 22.4cm, length 33.2cm, width 21.8cm

铜戈（M11:93）
战国
长 24.2 厘米

Bronze Ge
Warring States
Length 24.2cm

铜尊缶（M11:15）
战国
通高 38、口径 15、底径 13.7 厘米

Bronze Zunfou
Warring States
Height 38cm, rim diameter 15cm, base
diameter 13.7cm

石编磬（M11:52～64）

战国

长 19.6~48.6、宽 7.1~13.7、厚 2.1 厘米

A chime of sonorous stones

Warring States

Lengths 19.6-48.6cm, widths 7.1-13.7cm, thickness 2.1cm

东沟长岭楚墓群

Donggouchangling Chu cemetery

东沟长岭楚墓群位于淅川县仓房镇陈庄村东沟组东南的长岭上，丹江口水库西岸。2006年8~11月，河南省文物考古研究所、南阳市文物考古研究所对东沟长岭楚墓群进行了文物钻探和考古发掘，共发掘战国楚墓、汉代墓葬62座，车马坑5座，出土陶、铜、玉器等遗物400余件。

战国楚墓均为中小型土坑竖穴木椁墓，部分有长方形斜坡墓道，葬式多为仰身直肢葬，时代为战国中晚期；随葬品以陶器为主，其组合为鼎、敦、豆、壶，鼎、敦、豆、壶、盘、匜，鼎、敦、豆、壶、盘匜、小口鼎、浴缶、提梁盉等，另有部分铜器和玉器，如铜剑、戈、车軎、车辖及玉璧、玉珩等。

车马坑破坏严重，深不足1米，有的车马坑为两马一车，有的为四马二车，马背对车辕。车舆为长方形，两轮下有轮坑。

汉墓均为小型墓，随葬品主要为陶器，有仓、灶、井、猪及铜镜、铜钱等。

东沟长岭墓地的发掘，不仅对研究战国中晚期秦、楚两种文化的融合关系及楚墓的埋葬制度、文化特征等问题有一定的参考价值，也为这一地区汉墓的综合研究提供了有价值的考古资料。

铜马衔（M59:15、16）
战国
（上）长21厘米
（下）长22.2厘米

Bronze curb bits
Warring States
(upper) Length 21cm
(lower) Length 22.2cm

Donggouchangling Chu cemetery is located in Donggou village, Cangfang town in Xichuan county. Henan Provincial Institute of Cultural Relics and Archaeology, and Nanyang Municipal Institute of Cultural Relics and Archaeology excavated the cemetery from August to November of 2006. The excavation revealed 62 Chu and Han tombs, 5 chariot and horse pits, and collected more than 400 pottery, bronze and jade artifacts.

All the Chu tombs are medium and small shaft tombs. Some of them witness a rectangular slope passage. The majority of the occupants are an extended burial. They are dated to the middle and late Warring States period. Most of the funeral objects are pottery vessels. The compositions are a Ding tripod, a Dun, a Dou and a pot; a Ding tripod, a Dun, a Dou, a pot and a dish; a Ding tripod, a Dun, a Dou, a pot, a dish, a Ding tripod with small orifice, a Yufou, a You with over-top handle.

The chariot and horse pits were heavily damaged with less than one meter deep. Some chariot and harness pits witness two horses and one chariot, and others have four horses and two chariots. The back of horse is against the shaft of chariot. The carriage is rectangular. Under two wheels witness wheel pits.

The excavation at the Donggouchangliang cemetery provides valuable archaeological data for investigating the fusion between Qin and Han cultures in the late Warring States, and the burial system and cultural characteristics.

铜剑（M28:2）　　Bronze sword
战国　　　　　　　Warring States
长 33、宽 3.8 厘米　Length 33cm, width 3.8cm

后　记

　　2005年3月15日，河南省南水北调中线工程文物保护抢救工作正式启动。随着文物抢救工作的大规模展开和深入进行，在工程涉及的南阳、平顶山、许昌、郑州、焦作、新乡、鹤壁、安阳等八个省辖市的干渠和库区范围内，经过科学的考古发掘，相继发现了一大批重要的文物点，出土了一大批具有重要价值的精美文物。为了充分展示我省南水北调中线工程文物保护抢救工作取得的重大阶段性成果，回报各级领导、专家和社会各界对我们工作的关心和支持，我们从已实施发掘的100余处文物点出土的大批文物中，选择了价值重大、品相精美的近2000件文物，举办了《文明·水·责任——河南省南水北调中线工程考古成果展》，配合该展览，特出版了《河南省南水北调工程考古发掘出土文物集萃（一）》，以飨读者。

　　在展览举办和该书的编写过程中，陈爱兰局长、孙英民副局长、李玉东副局长等领导始终高度重视并热情指导。中国社会科学院考古研究所、河南省文物考古研究所、郑州市文物考古研究院、洛阳市文物工作队、安阳市文物考古研究所、新乡市文物考古研究所、南阳市文物考古研究所、鹤壁市文物工作队、许昌市文物工作队、濮阳市文物保护管理所、焦作市文物工作队、淇县文物保护管理所、重庆市文物考古研究所、郑州大学、武汉大学、四川大学、山东大学等承担有关文物保护抢救工作的单位积极配合，给予大力支持；河南博物院徐雷、李勤、刘璐同志为举办展览付出了辛勤劳动；河南省文物考古研究所胡永庆同志为该书的编辑做了大量工作，祝贺同志拍摄了该书所用照片，马萧林同志为该书做了英文翻译。在此，我们谨表谢忱！

河南省文物局南水北调文物保护办公室　编辑部

2008年6月

Postscript

The salvage conservation work of cultural relics in the Middle-line Project of Water Diversion from South to North in Henan province formally started On March 15, 2005. With the development of large-scale salvage work, large quantities of archaeological excavations have carried out in Nanyang, Pingdingshan, Xuchang, Zhengzhou, Jiaozuo, Xinxiang, Hebi, and Anyang cities, and unearthed a large number of exquisite artifacts. In order to show the result of salvage conservation for cultural heritage achieved in the past years and to express our sincere gratitude to the concern and support from leaders, experts, and all circles of the society, we have selected nearly 2000 valuable, exquisite artifacts recovered from more than 100 excavated sites or cemeteries, and held "Civilization, Water and Responsibility----Exhibition of Archaeological Achievement in the Middle-line Project of Water Diversion from South to North in Henan Province". We have specially edited the book, *Volume I for Selected Cultural Relics from Archaeological excavations* in the Conservation Project of Water Diversion from South to North in Henan Province, to present readers.

During the course of exhibition and edition, Mrs. Chen Ailan, director of Henan Provincial Administration of Cultural Heritage, Mr. Sun Yingmin, and Li Yudong, deputy directors of Henan Provincial Administration of Cultural Heritage, have emphasized and guided the work. The Institute of Archaeology, Chinese Academy of Social Sciences, Henan Provincial Institute of Cultural Relics and Archaeology, Zhengzhou Municipal Institute of Cultural Relics and Archaeology, Luoyang Municipal Team of Archaeology, Anyang Municipal Institute of Cultural Relics and Archaeology, Xinxiang Municipal Institute of Cultural Relics and Archaeology, Nanyang Municipal Institute of Cultural Relics and Archaeology, Hebi Municipal Team of Archaeology, Xuchang Municipal Team of Archaeology, Puyang Municipal Conservation Institute of Cultural Relics, Jiaozuo Municipal Team of Archaeology, Qixian Conservation Institute of Cultural Relics, Chongqing Municipal Institute of Cultural Relics and Archaeology, Zhengzhou University, Wuhan University, Sichuan University, Shandong University and so on, have actively cooperated and support the work. Mr. Xu Lei, Mrs. Li Qin, and Ms. Liu Lu from Henan Museum have contributed their arduous work for this exhibition. Mr. Hu Yongqing from Henan Provincial Institute of Cultural Relics and Archaeology has done much work for the editing work. Mr. Zhu He from Henan Provincial Institute of Cultural Relics and Archaeology took all the photographs in this book. Mr. Ma Xiaolin form Henan provincial Institute of Cultural Relics and Archaeology translated the book into English. We wish to thank all the agencies and individuals.

Office for the Conservation of Cultural Relics from Water Diversion from south to North,
Henan Provincial Administration of Cultural Heritage
June 2008